MARRIAGE
FIRE CODE

Fernando Villicaña

To Tim & Hedi. May you
both be blessed as you read
this book.
Matt 19:6
Fernando Villicaña
10/17

Printed in the United States of America

First Printing, 2017

ISBN 978-1-54391-092-6

Firehouse Church
915 W. Imperial Hwy #170
Brea, California 92821

www.MarriageFireCode.com

Dedication

I dedicate this book to my incredible wife Elizabeth, my first and only love of my life. Without whom, I would not be able to pen the joys, lessons and experiences of a married life. Since 1976 we have journeyed together in marriage and ministry - always and forever.

Acknowledgements

A HUGE THANK you to all my friends of Praise Chapel Christian Fellowship whom I have had the privilege of knowing for the past 30 plus years and the leadership and members of Firehouse Church, Brea. I am grateful and honored to labor for Christ alongside such a wonderful group of associate church pastors sent out from the Firehouse Fellowship - Eric and Veronica Salas (PC Norwalk, CA), Johnny and Christy Caldera (PC Hollywood FL), Josiah and my youngest daughter Marie Silva (Freedom House Fullerton, CA), Martin and Kelly Tudon (PC/New Life Goodlettsville TN), Felix and Pricilla Fanti (PC Palm Desert, CA), Gilbert and Patti Castillo (Faith Alive Westminster, CA), and Evangelist Javier Gaitan (Hayward, CA). A special thanks to our Assistant Pastors Richard and Maria Knudtson who have worked tirelessly with me in the ministry for the past 25 plus years.

I am forever grateful to my friend and brother Steve Lagos who led me to the Lord January 18, 1974 from a powerful church in Sepulveda, California and the late Pastor Samuel C. Meza who was my very first Pastor. A special thanks to Pastor Mike and Donna Neville from whom I acquired the spiritual tools and experience necessary to pastor my church as well as navigate successfully through the challenges of married life. The call of God upon my life was realized through their selfless investment in my life and ministry. And last but not least my three children Vanessa, Aaron and Marie who have been among the greatest joys of my life and ministry. To my eldest daughter Vanessa, it was your constant encouragement that allowed for this book to finally see the light.

Table of Contents

Introduction

MY SINCERE PRAYER is that in reading this book you will gain insight into the timeless principles given us by God Himself concerning marriage. In addition, I offer my 26 plus years of experience serving Firehouse Church as the Senior Pastor, providing marital counseling, teaching, and preaching the word of God on the subject as well as drawing from my own 40 plus years of marriage.

Wouldn't we expect the one who created the institution of marriage to dictate concerning it? Would God give us the unity of marriage and leave us to wonder how to live in it? God has said quite a bit on the subject of marriage and we would be wise to pay careful attention to it. In this book, we will carefully examine timeless principles that if adhered to will greatly increase your chances of a successful and fulfilled marriage.

Family values. Here's a term we've heard thrown around a lot in the past few years. The debate of what constitutes a "family" is now at the forefront of political circles. Some of the new and novel interpretations of what defines a family is concerning to say the least. Our culture is conjuring up new interpretations of what right and wrong is, what morality is. Being faithful to one wife, one husband, one family, as God's original and unchanging institution of marriage, is under attack today. It's little wonder then, that a recent Gallup poll found that 73% of those under 45 regarded the idea of being committed to one person for life as being "useless and unworkable." The breakdown of the family has had a major impact on our nation's problems, specifically in the areas of teenage pregnancy, teenage suicide, abortion, drugs, gang involvement, and poverty even. The further we get from the basic scriptural truth of the family, the more we see crisis,

1

chaos, and crime. The issue of crime is a relational one! Think about it, if you don't respect your neighbor's privacy, chances are, you'll probably violate it.

If you have little or no moral values, your behavior can easily be one of violation. If you are deprived of love, you cannot have other people's best interest at heart, which may lead to self-destruction or destructive behaviors toward others. The only way to find our way out of this impending crisis is to return to the simplicity of God's plan of a man and woman being joined together to form a new team called family. Simple yet profound.

People get married and simply don't live by the vows that they made. It seems that some people have rewritten these sacred vows in this generation: instead of for better or for worse," it's "until it gets more difficult."; Instead of "in sickness and health," it's "until you cease to meet my needs."; and instead of "for richer or poorer till death do us part," it's "as long as we have money, or until someone better comes along, I pledge my life to you.

"Forsaking all others," "sacrifice," and "submit" are words being removed from a lot of ceremonies today. I married a couple where the woman requested to have her name announced first and that any reference to "weaker vessel" or "submission" not be mentioned. She asked if I could use only portions of scripture and omit the complete version which referred to these things. Coming into a marriage with this kind of attitude sets you up for failure because God has set certain things in order for a reason. He created male and female differently and assigned different roles. The groom in this wedding ceremony didn't care about his bride's requests so long as he got the honeymoon! The real problems came after the honeymoon unfortunately, and they are no longer together. When asked why they wanted to dissolve their marriage, the husband told me that their roles have been completely reversed. A failure to recognize and affirm God's teaching could be devastating. I invite you to take this journey with me as we look at God's original design for marriage.

Chapter 1
In The Beginning

God's Intention for Marriage

MARRIAGE ISN'T ALWAYS easy. Sometimes it seems easier to fall in love than to stay in love. For that reason, more and more couples are willing to throw in the towel and walk away from their marriages rather than put forth an honest effort to learn how a marriage can thrive. However, there is light at the end of the tunnel. Your marriage really can be one of the greatest joys of your life. With a willingness to change and a commitment to adhere to timeless and proven principles given us through the word of God, you can share a positive, rich, intimate, and deeply satisfying life with your spouse. We live in a culture that has become open to anyone's interpretation of what a marriage should be and where traditional views are looked upon as irrelevant, archaic even. In the midst of such trend however, God has not left us wandering. Instead, He reaches out to us with a wonderful plan and purpose for marriage. The scripture says *"In the beginning, God created..."*

This is huge. God, the creator of heaven, earth, and everything in between, has reached out and given us clear direction as to what healthy marriages look like. Part of God's creation was man, woman and the joining of the two (AKA marriage/holy matrimony). Most marriages today are anything but holy. Couples tend to say and do things to one another that undermine what was originally designed to be purposeful and fulfilling. Trial and error is unavoidable and will always be part of life, but I have always believed that it can be dramatically reduced if we simply obey God and acquire the tools necessary

3

to navigate through the rough waters of life. I read a marriage book recently where the author wrote; "People don't have marriage problems, they have God problems." I believe that. The old saying "you can be so heavenly minded you're no earthly good" is false. The truth is that the more "heavenly minded" we are, the better off we would be here on earth. Our vertical relationship with God will greatly affect our horizontal relationships with people. The Bible says:

> Then the Lord God took the man and put him in the garden of Eden to tend and keep it. And the Lord God commanded the man, saying, "Of every tree of the garden you may freely eat; And the Lord God said, "It is not good that man should be alone; I will make him a helper comparable to him." Then the rib which the Lord God had taken from man He made into a woman, and He brought her to the man. And Adam said: "This is now bone of my bones and flesh of my flesh; She shall be called Woman, because she was taken out of Man."
> - Genesis 2:15,16,18,22, & 23, NKJV

When God describes man's responsibility as one who would tend or cultivate the garden, it doesn't mean that Adam was called to be some kind of glorified gardener. The word "tend" actually meant Adam's job in the Garden was to "take care of and guard" it. Adam obviously dropped the ball at one point, and we are still paying the price for that failure today. We are called to do the same thing Adam was charged to do, take care of and guard those things within our sphere of influence, namely our marriage and family.

God's first intention for marriage is a very practical one, to fill the void produced by isolation, and provide fellowship, closeness and intimacy. We are all hardwired with a need for companionship, it is in fact one of life's greatest needs. In the movie *Cast Away*, actor Tom Hanks (a FedEx executive) was forced to transform himself physically and emotionally to survive a crash landing on a deserted island. After being on the island alone over a period of time, he ends up building a one-sided relationship with a volleyball he named "Wilson." The point again is this: we have been created with a need for other people, relationships.

Without such, well… I'm not sure if this means that in his loneliness Adam would have ended up painting a face on a coconut and pouring his heart out to it. However, we do read that he named *all* the animals. God's purpose of creating male and female (marriage) was (and is today) to close the gap of loneliness, a feeling of isolation and to share with one another.

That's why God said,

> "It is not good for the man to be alone; I will make him a helper suitable for him"
> - Genesis 2:18

After observing and naming all the animals, Adam must have experienced some degree of loneliness and isolation so God created woman to fill that void. A void that cannot be met by a volleyball, a pet, or anything else for that matter. Another reason revealed in scripture for marriage is to be a reflection of God's image. God said,

> "Let Us make man in Our image, according to Our likeness…God created man in His own image, in the image of God He created him; male and female He created them"
> - Genesis 1:26-27

Marriage should reflect God's image to a lost and dying world. Because we're created in the image of God, people who wouldn't otherwise know what God is like should be able to see Him through us. Another reason for marriage found in Genesis is to have children. God told Adam to "be fruitful and multiply," a command I'm sure Adam gladly obeyed. It was, and is today, God's intention to have people pass on to their children the life lessons and relationship that comes through knowing the Lord. If this mission is not fulfilled, it creates a vacuum.

> When all that generation had been gathered to their fathers, another generation arose after them who did not know the Lord nor the work which He had done for Israel
> - Judges 2:10

It is every parent's responsibility to do their part in safeguarding the next generation from living outside of a knowledge of God and His statutes. My wife Liz and I have always tried to keep this purpose in mind as we raised our children. Have we had hiccups and disappointments along the way? Sure, we have. But this never stopped us from striving to produce children who continue to learn and live by solid principles. We parents must do our very best in creating an atmosphere in our homes that is conducive to God's Spirit moving freely.

The things of God should not be a novelty but commonplace in our homes. If children do not embrace a spiritual mission as they grow up, they may live their entire lives without experiencing the privilege of God using them in a significant way. Each marriage is critically important as it sets the stage for a future full of promise and purpose.

Leaving and Cleaving

Therefore a man shall leave his father and mother and
cleave to his wife, and they shall become one flesh
- Genesis 2:24

Leaving home and cleaving with your spouse is so very basic, yet failure to do so is the root of much of the marital problems encountered today. You will never fully *cleave* until you *leave*. If there is a failure in practicing this principle, it can wreak havoc on marriages and throw things off kilter. Failure to leave and cleave is out of God's order of things, and like any other area of our lives, we end up confused and frustrated outside of God's original design for us. Let me make it simple: marriage begins with a leaving! Paraphrased: *"Leave your mother and father to go and start a family of your own."* That's not to say that once you get married you're not the son or daughter of your parents, or that you should dishonor your parents through abandonment, but to recognize that a new family has begun and your primary loyalty is now directed towards each other.

Whenever a young married couple asks my opinion on whether or not they should live with their parents, I tell them I think it's a bad idea. Most couples do so for economic reasons. Young couples who usually do not plan ahead and rush into a marriage are almost forced into moving in with family. I think you are better off living in that tiny little apartment or room and get to know each other as husband and wife with your own privacy than live with parents. Every young couple needs space to make those critical relational adjustments without having parents or in-laws listening in and giving input to their problems. Issues need to be ironed out on your own. That's part of maturity and growth. Besides that, intimacy is a very important part of your bonding and is often spontaneous. This needs to be valued. A young couple's intimate time together should not have to be adjusted around other people's schedules. Usually, when a couple does move in with parents (or anyone else for that matter) they usually end up regretting it and have to play catch up to repair patterns and habits formed by not being able to freely express themselves or rely on one another rather than their parents.

Many of the husbands and wives we have counseled end up resenting their spouses for placing them in awkward situations. The wife who has to live with in-laws usually have problems that surface for years to come. It has been my experience that men expect their new wives to love his parents the same way he does, and it rarely (if ever) works that way. He needs to get away from Mom and make you his wife and go-to person! If the husband fails to do this, he places undue pressure on his wife and adds a huge stress to a relationship that needs as much concentrated time with each other as possible. Wives can easily do the same. I remember the first year or two of my marriage having to deal with my wife relying on her mother for resources that I could not provide at the time. It really added pressure on me and systematically produced in me a sense of inadequacy and sometimes failure. If there was something extra that Liz wanted that we could not afford at the time, she would call Mom who always came through for her. I don't think there is anything wrong visiting regularly, receiving gifts from time to time, or going shopping with Mom occasionally. However, if it gets to a point where it becomes habitual or she still depends on her mother for things, it can undermine critical elements of relationship building between husband and wife. Cut the apron strings!

> For this reason a man will leave his father and mother and be united to his wife, and they will become one flesh.
>
> - Genesis 2:24, NIV

"For this reason..." What reason? Let's go back one verse - verse 23: *"... she is now bone of my bones, And flesh of my flesh..."* You are one now! Neither he or she should be placed in a position to have to compete with friends or family members for your time. The husband and wife relationship ought to be closer than brothers, closer than sisters, and even closer than parent and child. I have two daughters, both of which I have released to marriage. I will admit it was difficult at first. For a loving father to release his daughter to the care of another man can be concerning. Will he care for her and treat her well, provide for her, love her etc. Even with those concerns, Liz and I have determined to release them from our immediate covering, and give them space to learn and grow together as a married couple. We have taught them to make a healthy shift from us to their husbands and work out their problems without having to run to either of us as an escape from their responsibility to find solutions. Are we there for them? Of course we are, and always will be.

But we have allowed our daughters to adjust their dependency upon us to "him," their own husbands. In fact, we have encouraged all of our children who have married to leave and cleave, and they understand it well. Husbands, *"...she is your companion and your wife by covenant."* (Malachi 2:14b). The word for companion in Hebrew could be translated as "one, united in thoughts, goals, plans, and efforts." We are to be united with each other in thoughts, goals, plans, and efforts. Paul tells husbands

> "You husbands likewise, live with (your wives) in an understanding way, as with a weaker vessel, since she is a woman; and grant her honor as a fellow heir of the grace of life, so that your prayers may not be hindered.
> - 1 Peter 3:7

This verse is telling husbands that if we don't make the wife top priority it can actually hinder your communication with God (prayer life). What is a husband to do? Live with your wife with understanding and honor her. To dwell with means to be aligned to. It means to place honor upon or to give maintenance to. Remember, just as Adam was told, we must tend our garden. Consistent upkeep is the key. Your marriage needs maintenance, and needs for attention or weeds will begin to pop up. Your marriage won't survive on cruise control.

If your marriage is going sour, someone is ignoring God's principles. Cleaving is an important word too, it means to stick, adhere or to be attached by a strong tie. It's more than being stuck together, it means a determined action, like a rock climber hanging on for dear life, something you're holding on to, clinging on to. Cleaving to your wife, your husband - inseparable! Cemented or glued together. Why does the scripture seem to target the husband? *"For this cause shall a man leave his mother and father."* *"Husbands, dwell with your wives according to knowledge"*

Well, because the main responsibility of the marriage rests on the husband! Men, it falls on your shoulders, and your main concern and effort should now be on growing your marriage. Leaving your parents means recognizing that your marriage created a new family, and that this new family must be a higher priority than your previous family. As mentioned prior, God has a wonderful plan for your marriage but expects us to tap into His anointing (His ability that goes beyond our ability) and lead our families to spiritual health. Oh, that we may fulfill the will of God and be what God meant us to be. Is your spouse your best friend? Are you honoring one another?

Are you more concerned about your spouse's health and well-being than you are yours? Great advice, if you would love your partner more than you do yourself, you will bring out the best in them. Love truly conquers all.

The Marriage Miracle

So then, they are no longer two but one flesh. Therefore what God has joined together, let not man separate."

- Matthew 19:6

By the way, that includes attorneys! What does it mean to be one? It can't just mean physically, there are two separate people we're dealing with. It can't mean sexually, almost anyone can join themselves sexually and not be in unity and can be considered far from being one. In order to fully appreciate and experience oneness, we should first understand the meaning of two becoming one. When Jesus made this statement (two becoming one) He was pointing out two things mentioned earlier: 1) Leaving; and 2) Cleaving.

One of the dictionary definitions of the word "cleave" is to adhere to, to become very strongly involved with or emotionally attached to (someone). When spiritually wrought by God, "cleaving" molds two people into one person. This is what I would refer to as the *marriage miracle*. A miracle is something out of the ordinary, something supernatural, a surprising and welcome event that is inexplicable by natural or scientific laws and is therefore considered to be the work of a divine agency (God) that yields very welcome consequences. Marriage (holy matrimony) between the husband and wife become *spiritually* united by God, they become meshed into one being. Each grows into the very being of the other. They become one body, one flesh, one person. So, "the two shall be one" refers to a spiritual bond (supernatural), an emotional bond (empathy, caring), and a mental bond (thinking, knowing, anticipating…).

This is cleaving in the greatest sense of the word. It is this "cleaving" or unity that brings the best out of both people to create a new creature—from *me* and *you*—to *us*. In most of the wedding ceremonies I perform, I talk about the miracle of marriage. "The marriage of two believers is like when you accept Jesus Christ as your Lord and Savior," you are joined with Him, you become a new creation/person, old things are passed away and behold, all things become new. When you get married, scripture says that the two shall be one flesh. Not one in purpose alone, but one in soul, spirit, physical intimacy, goals, mindset, and as one you go forward together in love and life. Something holy takes place by the Spirit of God inside of a man and a woman who decide to commit themselves to each other and God for life. It certainly is a precious thing in the sight of God.

Marriage is Sacred

There are many things about who we are that could be considered sacred. One of the things that is sacred is our sexuality, and therefore should not be violated. Sex is sacred, and marriage is sacred; both need to be maintained with particular boundaries. Temptations stalk all of us every single day in one way or another. Does this have anything to do with loving your spouse? No! You can love your spouse 100% and still struggle with lust. The human body responds to sight, entertained by our imagination which gives you all kinds of false hints that stolen waters are going to be sweeter than the one you are drinking, but they are not. They leave you emptier. So, the simple fact that you are tempted should never justify the act of immorality or violate the sanctity of marriage. And that goes across the board in all expressions of our sexuality, married or single. When God created man and woman, it was His plan, not our plan. When God said in Genesis *"it is not good for man to be alone,"* he meant it. God was with Adam and walked with him in the cool of the garden. Yet, God created the charm, beauty and the complementary nature of woman in a way that made it possible for her to meet the emotional needs of man. This is something that God put only in her. The two then make a commitment for life. This is the design of Almighty God. For all who claim to be a believer and follower of Jesus Christ, there then should be a certain code of doctrine and conduct to adhere to. There is belief and expression of that belief that should be experienced. In all we do, it should never impugn the character of God as He works through us.

The Christian life is filled with identifying the order of God and bringing oneself to a place of obedience to that order. If we keep the sanctity of marriage on our minds and in our hearts, we will then experience the fullness of that relationship. Marriage (as God has given it to us) is the most sacred relationship you will ever enter into. Although there is only one word for love in English, there are four words for love in the Greek language: agape, phileo, storge and eros. Agape is God's love, phileo is friendship love, storge is protective love, and eros is romantic love.

Marriage is the only thing that brings these four loves together. If you remove agape from any of the other loves, the depth of each erodes. Eros (romantic love) becomes redefined without the love of God.

The relationship between the believer and God is Biblically likened to that of a bride and her groom. The sanctity of relationship between God and man as well as between a man and a woman in the sacred act of marriage is reflected in the singular commitment to one another. When you say "I do" to one, you are essentially saying "I won't" to all others. So, any departure from the purity and sacredness of marriage as defined biblically is to compromise the fullness that it provides, and thus not acceptable in the sight of God.

Marriage Fire Code

Please take time to pray this prayer:

> Lord God, I realize that my spouse and I are wonderfully made. I pray that you will remind me of the marriage miracle, that two have become one. Help me to honor my marriage covenant by leaving my mother and father and cleaving to my spouse. Help me to recognize my spouse as a gift from God and to treat my spouse accordingly. Lord, I am committed to live my life under your divine order and honor your word and direction above all else. Help me to live a morally righteous life and never be unfaithful to you or my spouse. I release my children to your care in every stage of their lives and promise to raise them and lead them in such a way that will honor you. I pray all of this in the name of my Lord and Savior Jesus Christ. Amen.

Chapter 2
Maintaining Oneness

Blending

PICTURE WITH ME a bag of tea being placed into a cup of hot water. The water changes color because it draws out of the tea the various herbs and spices. Marriage is like the water in the cup. Good or bad, there is no denying that whatever is inside will come to the surface, especially when the heat is on. The same with a sponge, whatever is inside will surface when pressure is added. When you immerse a man and a woman into the marriage relationship, whatever is in them is drawn out. Their character, qualities, gifts, talents, and the positive attributes come out in marriage like no other time. At the same time though, the negative attributes come out as well. The weaknesses, tempers, attitudes are also drawn out. Marriage truly brings out the best and the worst in us. What if we don't blend very well? If I took the tea bag and said "I don't really like this, I'm going to go find me another cup of water," and dipped that same bag into another cup of hot water, what will happen? Same results!

The point is, it's not the water that needs changing. It's not the water that causes the bad flavor or whatever it is I don't like, it's what's in the bag that has to change. A lot of times we don't like what we experience in our marriage relationship. So, we think that if we get a new cup (a new relationship) things are going to be better. Yet, we find the same things drawn out one more time. In the past 25 years of my pastoral ministry, I have seen scores of marriages fail for this same reason. The grass is always greener on the other side syndrome. The truth is, the grass is always greener whenever it is watered.

People feel that the answer to their problems is change the environment when the answers lie with the person. It is the *tea bag* not the water that determines the flavor of the tea. Let's ask God to change the inside.

Years ago, we used to sing a song in church that went like this: "Jesus on the inside, working on the outside oh what a change in my life." Unfortunately, someone changed the lyrics to "Jesus on the inside working on the outside, oh what a change in my *wife*." If we ask God to change what is in the inside of the bag, then we will be able to enjoy a good cup of tea (marriage).

The Law of Attachment

Almost everyone has seen Bob Clark's 1983 film, *A Christmas Story*. It is the story that features two young brothers during Christmas time. The eldest of the two brothers was "triple dared" by a school mate to place his tongue on a freezing metal flag pole in the school yard. It was from this experience that he learned something about the law of attachment and ultimately the pain of separation. The pole had become part of the boy and the boy became a part of that pole. The Lord declares in His Word that when two people come together in Holy Matrimony, they miraculously become one (attached).

> "and the two are united into one.' Since they are no longer two but one."
>
> - Mark 10:8, NLT

That's why the separation of that union, intimacy, trust is so painful. It's like the tongue being removed from that freezing flag pole. Why is that? Because attachments/ relationships are among our greatest needs in life. The best analogy used by God to describe our relationship with Him is as one in a marriage (He is the groom, we are His bride). During creation, the only thing that God said was not good was that man was left alone. Everything else was good in His eyes. In physics, the second law of thermodynamics is known as the *law of entropy*. It states that "things that are isolated move towards deterioration." Entropy operates spiritually and relationally as well. Whatever is cut off from the original source tends to deteriorate.

This is why oneness and unity is so crucial in marriage, anything less than a healthy shared relationship leads to separation and eventually pain. The enemy of our souls works through spiritual entropy (separation, roommates, conflict and eventually, divorce). As referred to in the previous chapter, there is really no life without relationships (Tom Hanks/Wilson). I believe that's what God was doing when He ordained marriage.

At the same time, few things can bring the best and the worst out of us like our life partner. The Lord declares in His Word that when two people (opposite sex) come together in Holy matrimony, they miraculously become one (attached). That's why the separation of love, intimacy and trust is so painful (think about the little boy's tongue being separated from the frozen metal pole). I read a story of a Christian couple that had been married 39 years. They'd been through some stormy times, but in their tenth-year marriage came the bout to end all bouts. The wife got so mad she pulled her suitcase out of the bedroom closet and started packing. "What are you doing?" her husband demanded. "I'm leaving." So without a word he got his suitcase and started filling it with his clothes. "Now, what are you doing?" his wife asked, bewildered. "If you're leaving," he told her firmly, "I'm going with you." If we're to make our marriages strong & pleasing to God, we have to commit to *"going where they go, staying where they stay, and dying where they die" (Ruth)*.

The idea of this type of commitment can be best symbolized by the ring married people wear on their fingers. The Christian custom of placing a wedding ring on the third finger began with the Greeks. The early Greeks (not Christians) believed that a certain vein, the "vein of love," ran from the third finger directly to the heart. Why they thought that no one knows... However, when you put those rings on each other's ring finger, part of you are symbolically saying that you want to be tied right into their hearts. You want to be committed to each other. Now, when the early Christians exchanged rings, they worked their way across the hand beginning with the index finger and ending with the ring finger. The groom first placed the ring on the tip of the bride's index finger, praying "in the name of the Father," moved it to her middle finger saying, "in the name of the Son," and finally, with the words "and of the Holy Spirit, Amen," he slipped the ring on the to the ring finger. In the giving of the ring, the early Christian was saying that the marriage would begin with a commitment to God.

Oneness Setbacks

There can be a myriad of issues that can cause setbacks in a marriage. I will cover just a few. The *first* thing that sinks a marriage is false expectations. I love what Ruth Graham, Evangelist Billy Graham's wife wrote: "I pity the married couple who expect too much from one another. It's foolish to expect from one another that which only Jesus Christ can be—always ready to forgive, totally understanding, unendingly patient, invariably tender and loving, unfailing in every area, anticipating every need, making more than adequate provision. Such expectations put a marriage under an impossible strain." You cannot expect your spouse to be perfect or to meet all of your needs. Expectations come in all shapes and sizes. In our pre-marriage coaching course, we outline three marriage myths that need to be recognized in order to develop healthy expectations. These falsehoods, when carried into a marriage, can jeopardize oneness.

Myth #1: We expect the same things from marriage.

Generally speaking, I suppose we do. Things such as love, peace, joy, prosperity, unity, fun etc. But in reality, we all have our own pre-conceived ideas of what we want out of marriages, most of which are how our needs are going to be met. The expectations from one partner to another to have those needs met are usually different however.

Myth #2: Everything bad will disappear.

Not so, if anything, these deficiencies are magnified in marriage. They don't just magically go away because we are "in love." That is why it is so important to identify your weaknesses and iron them out the best you can prior to marriage.

Myth #3: My spouse will make me whole.

The old "you complete me" quote from the movie *Jerry Maguire* as cute and touching as it is false. When you are single, you are not a "half" looking for another half to make you whole. When God created you as an individual, He did so with the capacity for wholeness. The bottom line is this, if you try to build intimacy with a person before you have done the basic work of getting whole, all your relationships become an attempt to fill voids. On an everyday basis, we are exposed to false images and models for couples that set us up for a sense of inadequacy and develop false expectations. These influences often place a huge pressure on today's women to compete with images like the Kardashians—always made up, shaped up and dressed to kill. News flash: reality TV is not reality. If you don't believe that, just look into the real lives of most of these "stars" and you will learn that many of their lives are in utter turmoil. They aren't reality shows, they are more like fantasy shows.

If you are expecting your husband or wife to measure up to the false image portrayed by the media, you are setting yourself up for unrealistic expectations that are bound to end in frustration and failure. Decisions need to be made on reality and character rather than the bling or pizzazz (style, flash, flair). When the smoke clears and you find yourself married to a real human being with all of his or her limitations and faults, that's when true love shines. It is the reality of love and the commitment you made as you exchanged vows that will carry you through years of marriage. Listen carefully, if your decision to marry is based on outward appearances and you expect everything to go perfectly, you are setting yourself of for a huge disappointment. *False* expectations will lead to *frustration.*

The *second* setback in marriages today is selfishness. They may not recognize it at the time, but most struggling couples that I counsel deal with this one issue. Selfishness is at the core of almost every major marital problem there is. Think about it for a moment. If there is infidelity and cheating going on, the root of that sin is selfishness. At the heart of most major marital battles is a spouse who demands that things be done their way, and is not willing to compromise. This is selfishness. How many times have we heard one of these statements along with a threat to separate or divorce: "I'm not getting what I want out of this marriage," "You never...you always...," "I didn't sign up for this," "I want... I don't want...I don't feel..." Me, me, me, I, I, I—selfishness! The word "selfishness" is by definition: lacking consideration for others;

concerned chiefly with one's *own* personal profit or pleasure. The Bible tells us:

"Let each of you look not only to his own interests, but also to the interests of others."

- Philippians 2:4, ESV

Ladies, if you find a husband who loves you more than himself, you have a future with him. That is what brings the best out of each other. Whatever is important to you must become important to him. A good marriage is one where you care for each other and find fulfillment in that. The God who created us gives us this instruction: "Don't be selfish." Trust me, selfishness is a killer of marriages. A selfish person is one who lacks concern for the values of others or does not see the need to return a value for a value. A selfish person is one who acts for his own sake, one whose actions are directed to benefit oneself. It fights a common goal and emphasizes only what benefits you.

It's all about my needs, my wants, my time, my money, my feelings, and my life. Looking out for #1 with little or no regard for the other is a oneness killer. Remember: love your spouse *more* than you do yourself and you will bring the best out of them. Love is about giving, not always receiving.

For all the men out there, you will find your greatest sense of fulfillment when you love, put your wife first, provide and be a covering for your wife. That is how God intended it to be. I have found that many many husbands battle with this, particularly the younger ones. In order to live out a marriage the way God intended it to be, you must remember that whatever is important to your wife must become a top priority to you. We must all fight a spirit of selfishness.

Why? Because love ventilates itself through giving. Healthy, happy relationships are based on caring, cooperation, and commitment. Selfishness, or being overly concerned with just your needs, wants, and feelings prevents you from holding up your end of a mutually satisfying relationship. Many people don't recognize when they're being selfish because they operate inside a bubble of me-first thoughts and practices. Putting yourself first becomes a habit. A selfish person is constantly looking for opportunities to put yourself center stage. You spend very little time listening because your focus is on pulling attention back to you. Eventually this way of thinking pushes

18

others away from you. In your intimate relationship, it creates hurt and resentment. Here are six indicators that you are being self-seeking or selfish:

1) You like being in control and find it difficult to compromise.
2) Giving and sharing do not come easily to you.
3) Putting your partner's needs first - before your own - is very difficult.
4) You hear constructive criticism as personal attacks.
5) You become moody when others have the spotlight.
6) Forgiving others is difficult.

The good news is that there is also no gene for selfishness; it's a learned behavior. That means like any other bad habit, it can be unlearned. Make a conscious effort to shift your focus from *me first to we first.*

The *third* setback that fights oneness in your marriage is a lack of good communication. Not sure where this illustration came from but I love it. A woman went to a judge and told him "I want to divorce my husband."

The judge said, "Do you have any grounds?" She said, "No, but we do own a half acre in Big Bear." The judge said, "I mean, do you have a grudge?" She said, "No, we park the car in front of the house." The judge said, "Does your husband beat you up?" She said, "No, I always get up before he does." Frustrated the judge said, "Why do you want a divorce?" She said, "He doesn't know how to communicate."

Does that describe the outcome of some conversations you have with your significant other? Sometimes it seems like we are on two completely different wavelengths. And we always blame our spouse for the misunderstandings and poor communication. One of the major complaints we husbands hear from wives is "he doesn't talk to me." Even if it's just "pillow talk." The problem, as Dr. Dobson writes it, is that God gave every woman 10,000 words a day, and a man only 5,000 words a day. And the men are usually "worded out" by the time they get home from work. What does this tell us?

Men must make a conscious effort to communicate with their wives. Wives should understand our tendencies and try to meet us half way. When it comes to communicating, try to remember OHRC—Open, Honest, and Reliable Communication. I open almost all my counseling sessions with

OHRC. The reason this is so important is because you can't build on a lie or half-truth. If the couple being counseled is not open and honest, we are wasting each other's time.

Six Tips to Maintaining Oneness in Your Marriage

1. Develop a Relationship with God

This point will be repeated several times in this book because this one thing will not only make all the difference in your marriage but in everything else as well. Jesus Christ is already Lord of the universe, but He waits patiently to have you make Him Lord of your life and marriage through a personal relationship. The goal should be to develop a Christ-centered relationship with your spouse. Doing so creates a buffer between the two of you, and provides an invaluable resource during the most difficult times. When you build your marriage around God, Hewill speak into your lives as you encounter challenges as well as help you appreciate all He is already doing to bless you. This has been vital in my relationship with my wife. The truth is this: since we both revere and respect God more than we do anyone else in life (including each other), we are constantly aware of His presence and principles. In building your relationship with God, you should adopt His attributes. Walking with God and knowing His word guides us through our marriage. We need His help.

> "Unless the Lord builds the house, they labor in vain who build it."
>
> - Psalm 127:1

As you come to know that very real God, you will increasingly understand that He really does know what is best for you, and your marriage. For He is the One who created us male and female. He is the One who created our bodies and minds, and who specifically designed the differences between us and even the different ways men and women think and view the world around them. The Bible says:

> For we are God's masterpiece. He has created us anew in Christ Jesus, so we can do the good things he planned for us long ago.
>
> - Ephesians 2:10, NLT

God is creating a masterpiece with every stroke of his hand we are getting closer and closer to that finished product. The Great Creator made man and woman for one another. He certainly knows how we can best relate to one another in marriage better than all the psychologists and marriage counselors combined. Jesus spoke about a foundation for life, and how it is applicable to a couple building a home together:

> Therefore everyone who hears these words of Mine and acts on them, may be compared to a wise man who built his house on the rock. And the rain fell, and the floods came, and the winds blew and slammed against that house; and yet it did not fall, for it had been founded on the rock. Everyone who hears these words of Mine and does not act on them, will be like a foolish man who built his house on the sand. The rain fell, and the floods came, and the winds blew and slammed against that house; and it fell—and great was its fall.
>
> - Matthew 7:24–27

Here, Jesus was talking about the need to build your spiritual house on a solid foundation, and the way to support your life through constant obedience to God and His Word. When you build your house on that Rock, you can withstand the storms and the "currents" of your selfishness and shortcomings.

2. Don't Sweat the Small Stuff

Here is another nugget of wisdom that reminds me of my wife. Anytime I take things too seriously or become angry, she tells me "Fern, don't sweat the small stuff." There is actually a website that has books dealing with stress management, and one of the books is titled *Don't Sweat the Small Stuff . . . and It's All Small Stuff*, written by Richard Carlson. It is all about perspective. We must realize how important perspective is when working through the many challenges that a marriage produces as well as other life situations. Here's a few of my personal favorites from Carlson's book: 1) "An argument that happened while you were walking out the door on your way to work is no longer an actual argument, it's a thought in your mind"; 2) "We forget that life isn't as bad as we're making it out

21

to be. We also forget that when we're blowing things out of proportion, we are the ones doing the blowing"; 3) "Choose to be kind over being right and you'll be right every time"; 4) "Our disappointment comes about in essentially two ways. When we're experiencing pleasure, we want it to last forever. It never does. Or when we're experiencing pain, we want it to go away—now. It usually doesn't. Unhappiness is the result of struggling against the natural flow of experience"; and 5) "The first step in becoming a more peaceful person is to have the humility to admit that, in most cases, you're creating your own emergencies.

Life will usually go on if things don't go according to plan." Aren't these great? So, don't sweat the small stuff. I'm not sure if Liz got this term from a book or website, but almost every time I start stressing or become critical, her voice is there in my head reminding me not to major in the minors.

3. Learn to Control Your Anger

My gosh, this is a big one. Anger can be a killer of emotions, security, respect and love in a marriage. There will be no rekindling of the flame of love and passion if you are married to an angry person.

> A hot-tempered person starts fights; a cool-tempered person stops them
> > - Proverbs 15:18, NLT

> Short-tempered people do foolish things.
> > - Proverbs 14:17

Isn't that the truth. How many times have you or someone you know has made their worst mistakes or decisions while angry? I have said it many times: our prisons are full of people who have made just one bad decision, usually in a fit of rage. As a matter of fact, we are all just one decision away from peace or misery. Think of times in your life that your anger got the best of you, and you still regret it today. Learn to control your anger, you will blend so much better in your marriage. Anger management has been a huge topic in the past decade or so. Back in the day, we were just told to stop it.

Now we have learned that the goal of anger management is to reduce both your emotional feelings and the physiological arousal that anger causes.

I know, easier said than done, right? You can't get rid of, or avoid the things or the people that enrage you, nor can you change them, but you can learn to control your reactions. The first step is realization. Coming to grips with the fact that no good thing has ever come from anger. According to Jerry Deffenbacher, PhD, a psychologist who specializes in anger management, some people really are more "hotheaded" than others are; they get angry more easily and more intensely than the average person does. Research has also found that family background plays a role. Typically, people who are easily angered come from families that are disruptive, chaotic, and not skilled at emotional communications. This may be true, nevertheless this weakness must be dealt with and not written off as "something I was born with."

The Holy Spirit gives us the power to overcome those negative family influences. It's best to find out what it is that triggers your anger, and then to develop strategies to keep those triggers from tipping you over the edge. It may not come overnight. It is usually a long process, so be patient and take one step at a time. Notice I used the word "learn." Controlling your anger is an acquired ability. Control your anger before it controls you, as your marriage may depend on it. We will talk more about this in a later chapter titled "Guns N' Roses."

4. Watch What You Say

> Spouting off before listening to the facts is both shameful and foolish.
> - Proverbs 18:13

How many of us are guilty of that? I know I am. Liz catches me with this one more often than I would like to admit. The clear lesson here: the way to control anger is to control your mouth…your tongue (bridle/rudder)!

Anger is fueled by the words we speak. Whoever said "talk is cheap" couldn't be more wrong in this context. The *words we speak* (i.e. seeds planted in the minds and hearts of our spouse) reflect the thoughts and heart, and can change the course of your relationships. The words we speak are key to everything.

We can bless and curse with our words the consequences of which could be life-changing.

> A gentle answer deflects anger, but harsh words make tempers flare.
>
> — Proverbs 15:1

Nothing will reduce stress and tension in the home like getting control of your words. When you are angry or upset (and those times will come), *watch* what you say!

> "Be angry, and sin not!"
>
> — Ephesians 4:26

Anger is a normal human emotion/response to some situations, but must be controlled. The key is not allowing your anger to become a sin through some manifestation. Anger not dealt with turns to rage, and rage turns into murder. Maybe not literal murder, but a malicious desire to see the object of your anger suffer. Get a handle on your anger. Your life and the life of people brought into your madness depends on it. Again, our words are crucial and powerful. God rules His *world* with His *words*. Everything He does, He does with words: God spoke the world into existence. Repeatedly we read in the Bible "and God said…"

> *And God said*…let there be light and there was light.
>
> — Genesis 1:3 (Italics Mine)

He called Himself The Word.

> "In the beginning was the Word, and the Word was with God, and the Word was God…"
>
> — John 1:1

You would be surprised to learn how much change can be experienced by the words you speak. We are saved by words.

> "…and with the mouth confession is made unto salvation."
>
> — Romans 10:10

James devotes an entire chapter about the power of the tongue (i.e. spoken word).

> For we all stumble in many things. If anyone does not stumble in word, he is a perfect man, able also to bridle the whole body.
>
> - James 3:2

The level of success or failure in a marriage can be determined by the words we speak. Why is that? Because our speech is the product of our thoughts, which flow from the heart. Why are your thoughts so important? Because your thoughts become your speech, your speech determines what you do, and what you do will determine the level of your character and the quality of life you live.

> For as a man thinks in his heart, so is he.
>
> - Proverbs 23:7

So, the words we speak mark the birthplace for change, good or bad. We will cover this subject more extensively in another chapter.

5. Develop and Maintain a Good Sense of Humor

Here is another area of life that my wife Liz really helps me out with. She constantly reminds me not to take life too seriously. She smiles a lot and laughs for almost everything (or for nothing). It is spontaneous and contagious. Every once in a while, when I get too serious or intense about life, she will poke me and say, "Laugh." My response is "about what?" Then she will tell me, "Do you really need something to laugh about?" My answer is, "Yes, I do." Before you know it, we both start laughing and guess what, it works every time. It pulls me out of the tension that was stressing me out, and ends up making me feel better.

> A cheerful heart (laughter) does good like medicine, but a broken spirit makes one sick.
>
> - Proverbs 17:22

What is a broken spirit? Well, it means you've lost your vitality, your enthusiasm, and you're tempted to give up. On the

25

other hand, laughter is a gift God has given to us to release tension, and to keep our spirits from being broken (losing our zest). According to this verse, having a cheerful spirit is one of God's ways of keeping us healthy, emotionally and physically. Medical science has proven that when you laugh, chemicals and enzymes are released in the brain which are extremely important to the health of our vital organs. Listen to this finding from one of the articles in *Executive Digest*: "Scientists have been studying the effects of laughter on human beings and have found, among other things, that laughter has a profound and instantaneous effect on virtually every important organ of the human body. Laughter reduces unhealthy tensions, and relaxes the tissues, as well as exercising the most vital organs. Laughter, even when forced, results in beneficial effect on us, both mentally and physically.

So, the next time you feel nervous and jittery, indulge in a good laugh." I don't think I could ever possibly deal with the stresses and pressures of the ministry, if home were not a fun place to be. Have you ever started laughing and the people around you start laughing with you saying, "What's so funny?" not even knowing what it is you are laughing about? Laughter is both extremely contagious and healthy. I love to see and hear people I love laugh.

A merry heart makes laughter, but by sorrow of the heart the spirit is broken
- Proverbs 15:13

When a man is gloomy, everything seems to go wrong; when he is cheerful, it's like a continual feast!
- Proverbs 15:15

If you want your marriage to be a blessing and not a bondage, laugh a little more. It is an important part of maintaining oneness in your marriage.

6. Learn to Turn Setbacks Into Comebacks

Setbacks and letdowns have the potential to become a disaster for many people. Life can make you bitter or better, it's really a choice. If a person is not prepared to deal with a setback, it can become a permanent disaster. Although the great amount of success that you may be experiencing now will most likely continue in the future, here are six things you can do to make sure that you're covered when you experience a setback:

1) Identify what is and what isn't under your control.

It makes no sense to worry about things you can't change. Doing so only adds stress to a situation.

2) Replace negative thoughts with good thoughts.

This will help you move from bitter to better. How do you do this? (See below)

3) Learn to forgive offenses against you, then learn to forgive yourself.

First, don't hesitate to ask forgiveness if someone is offended by something you said or did. Once that is done and you have repented before God, don't rehearse it over and over in your mind. This will allow you to move forward, free from guilt or shame.

The way to turn a setback into a comeback is to have the attitude that even though nobody would ever want to repeat a bad circumstance again, you can learn from every mistake. As long as you are learning, you are growing. Some people just get older, while others mature. Your attitude will determine your altitude. Psychologists estimate that negative thoughts are seven times stronger than positive thoughts. That means that it takes seven positive thoughts to nullify one negative thought! The reason people have a hard time ridding themselves of negative thoughts and emotions is because they try to remove the thought or feeling without replacing it. That's like changing a flat tire without putting on a new tire. When a negative or bitter thought pops into your head immediately say to yourself "erase that and replace that." Then you replace the bitter thought with a better thought. The next time you find yourself in a situation that requires forgiveness say: "I made an honest mistake, and now I know better so I'll do better." The past is a place of reference; not a place of residence. Far too many people convict themselves over and over again for past mistakes and mishaps.

Remember, guilt always stifles a person. How many times have you held back from visiting a family member or not gone to a social gathering because there are unresolved issues between you and another person that you know will be there. Ask forgiveness (from the person and God), forgive yourself, then move on. Would a parent punish a teenager again and again for something the child did when he or she was seven-years-old? God the father wouldn't do that to you. So why would you want to continue to punish yourself in the present for an honest mistake you made in the past? You're only convicting the new and improved you, for something that the old you did. Give the new you a pardon. What it boils down to is learning from the past, then planning for a better you and a better future.

Another way to turn setbacks into comebacks is to remember that:

4) Someone's definition of you doesn't define you.

In 1979, as a sophomore in high school, a young basketball player was cut from the varsity team. He was devastated but he wasn't done. Three years later in 1982, he made the game winning shot in the NCAA championship. In 1984, he was passed over by the first two teams in the NBA draft, but went on to become arguably the greatest basketball player of all time. Michael Jordan epitomizes the fact that a person's opinion doesn't have to be your reality. Refuse to put on the jacket that someone wants to throw your way. Instead, *"put on the garment of praise for the spirit of heaviness."* You must not buckle under the pressure of having someone define who and what you are or are going to always be.

5) Failure is only permanent if you quit.

Here are some of my favorite quotes:

"Giving up is the only sure way to fail."
- Gena Showalter.

"There is no failure except in no longer trying."
- Chris Bradford.

"I have not failed. I've just found 10,000 ways that won't work."
- Thomas A. Edison.

"If you fail in any area of your marriage, get up and determine to beat that failure with another attempt."
- Fernando Villicaña.

These are all great quotes. Try to memorize some or all of these (especially the last one) so they can surface in a time of need.

6) New opportunities heal old wounds.

Has anyone you know ever been in a relationship that ended on a sour note? Perhaps the person was a little depressed, sitting around licking his or her wounds, and didn't feel like doing much. Finally, someone tells the person that he or she needs to get out of the house and go meet somebody new. And just like that, life starts to become fun again. It works the same way with temporary setbacks. So, when you experience a letdown, find a new opportunity to pursue as soon as you can. There is an expression: "When God closes a door, He opens a window." No matter whom you admire or aspire to be like, he or she has experienced some type of temporary setback. The powerful and prophetic words of Frederick Douglass remind us that "If there is no struggle, there is no progress. "If you want to travel the path of greatness that countless others have traveled before you, keep this in mind: Temporary setbacks and letdowns are learning experiences. Albeit tough learning experiences. But there is no reason for a temporary setback to turn into a permanent disaster. Instead, you can turn setbacks into comebacks.

Final Oneness Thought

Did you know that one of the greatest tools in God's toolbox to instill growth and maturity in your life is your spouse? There is absolutely no one God uses more than my wife to point out and help me with my character flaws and negative habits. She is also one of God's greatest tools to encourage and edify me. God uses your spouse more than any other tool in your life to help you grow spiritually.

The *fourth* setback in a marriage is unresolved issues. These are things that keep coming up over and over, no matter how much you try to avoid them. They could be finances, sex issues, in-laws, different views on disciplining your children, poor communication, and the list can go on and on. The worst unresolved issues aren't usually the ones that were created *in* your marriage; they are the ones you brought into your marriage! They manifest and are magnified when you live every day with someone. When you got married you weren't a blank slate. You brought with you a backpack of pain, disappointments, fears and habits from your previous life into marriage. The good news is that by taking the initiative to change, compromise, and work toward a healthy relationship, you can make a world of difference.

Please take time to pray this prayer:

> Lord Jesus, help me to blend with my spouse and not major in the minors. Help me see the good in everything and deal with the challenges of marriage with a sense of hope, faith and love. Remind me to bridle my tongue and deal with anger righteously and add value to my spouse in all that I do and say. I pray all of this in the name of my Lord and Savior Jesus Christ. Amen.

Chapter 3
Elements of a Healthy Marriage

ON JULY 29, 1981, one of the most highly publicized and glamorous weddings in history took place. Britain's Prince Charles married Lady Diana in a ceremony watched by an estimated audience of 750 million people worldwide. 4,500 pots of fresh flowers lined the route to St. Paul's cathedral. 2,500 people crowded that grand church where more than 75 technicians with 21 cameras worked to enable the world to watch this wedding. The United Kingdom made that day a national holiday to mark the wedding. For many people, this was a modern fairy tale. A royal prince weds a lovely lady in a grand cathedral surrounded by adoring subjects. They were the envy of millions. They were rich, young, handsome. It was said to be a "marriage made in heaven." Sadly, we know that the fairy tale quickly turned into a nightmare. The couple grew more and more distant. Affairs ensued. The storybook marriage "made in heaven" eventually collapsed into adultery and divorce.

The bottom line is that it takes more than a prince, a lady, and a palace to make a happy marriage. One of the main ingredients in the formula for a healthy marriage is regular maintenance. Marriages (as in all relationships) require effort. Many years ago, when I was studying for a promotion to Engineer in the Los Angeles City Fire Department, someone shared somethings with me that I have never forgotten. It was a simple formula which I have since applied to many areas of my life. My Captain asked me, "Do you want to be successful in the testing process?" To which I responded, "Of course I do." He grabbed a piece of chalk (a time before white boards) and began marking something on a huge chalk board behind him. He wrote a formula, $E=G$. I looked at it for a few seconds and asked "OK, what does that mean?" He answered, "Fernando, if you apply this formula to anything you do in life, it will pay off big for you." "Ok, ok, what does it mean?" I asked again. He told me, "Effort equals grade. The end result of whatever you do will be in direct proportion to the amount of effort you put into it." I have tried to apply this principle to every area of my life and share it with everyone I can.

"Let us not become weary in doing good, for at the proper time we will reap a harvest if we do not give up.

- Galatians 6:9, NIV

Well, marriages require a certain kind of effort.

Whatever you do, work heartily...
- Colossians 3:23a, ESV

Other verses read:

Work hard at whatever you do. You will soon go to the world of the dead, where no one works or thinks or reasons or knows anything.
- Ecclesiastes 9:10, CEV

"Live together in harmony and love, as though you only had one mind and spirit between you"
- Philippians 2:2, Phillips

Paul went on to write in Philippians that we have to do the right things to make a marriage (or any relationship) work. According to Philippians 2:2, God's ideal for your relationships is harmony, love and unity. The reality is that a lot of marriages today are in disharmony, conflict and disappointment. In my years of marriage counseling, I have encountered a staggering number of couples who have communicated disappointment in their marriage relationship. We hear things like, "I feel cheated by my marriage, I don't believe I have the power or energy to change the way things are, I have fallen out of love, we're no longer on the same page." What happened? Well, good marriages don't happen by osmosis.

It takes effort to make a marriage work. The good news is, you don't have to completely turn your life around to make your marriage better. Minor changes will go a long way and you can experience a revival in your marriage. Just remember, E=G.

How can we make our marriage work better? Ready for a huge revelation?

Element #1
Treat Each Other with Love and Respect

> "Nevertheless let each one of you in particular so love his own wife as himself, and let the wife see that she respects her husband.
>
> - Ephesians 5:33

Ladies, the Number *one* need of any man is *respect*. Believe it or not, this is more important than sex to him. You may say: "not my husband." A survey was taken where 400 men were given a choice between going through two different negative experiences. If they were forced to choose one of the following, which would they prefer to endure? a) To be left alone and unloved in the world or b) To feel inadequate and disrespected by everyone? The results were unanimous: the answer is "a." Most men would rather face isolation and not be loved than be disrespected. The above paragraph is an excerpt from *Love & Respect* by Dr. Emerson Eggerich. Do you want to know what the top four needs of men are? 1) honor and respect; 2) sex; 3) friendship with wife; and 4) support from his family. But the mega need for men is *respect*.

It is our oxygen. Men's egos can be big but actually quite fragile, and we need our wives to acknowledge us. The slightest look or tone that even hints disrespect or dishonor affects us more than we can ever admit to our wives. "It's not *what* you say, it's *how* you say it." Men have huge egos! Wives should learn how to use that fact to their advantage. "Wow honey, do you think you can carry that huge heavy bag from the car?" Husband comes into the house carrying three or four bags. He will do everything shy of getting a hernia proving that he is still strong and on top of his game.

You may say: "wait a minute, isn't that manipulation?" Maybe it is, but we just want to be your hero, it's actually a win-win situation, wouldn't you say? Most women don't understand how very important the need for honor is to a man. 1 Peter teaches that you can change your husband's ways without even opening your mouth. It talks about "...*the hidden person of the heart, with the incorruptible beauty of a gentle and quiet spirit, which is very precious in the sight of God.*" Gentle and quite is the opposite of rough and loud. Now, we men love the beauty of a woman. The Bible goes on to say: "*Do not let your adornment be merely outward—arranging the hair, wearing gold, or putting on fine apparel. Rather let it be the hidden person of the heart, (v3,4).* Although your beauty is appreciated, don't over emphasize how you look on the outside.

Let me shed some light about the depravity of our society. The more inwardly depraved a society is, the more externally focused they become.

In other words, the less you have going for you on the inside, the more you have to make happen on the outside. I'm not suggesting that you don't take care of yourself. I'm not saying that you shouldn't look nice. I really appreciate how my wife Liz looks, she is beautiful on the outside, but God emphasizes the inside qualities that count so much more. Contrary to the image that Hollywood portrays, what makes you most attractive to a man is your soul and spirit. Now, carnally speaking, some would disagree with that. But the truth is, the value over a long-term relationship is not physically based, but spiritually based. Have you ever met a good-looking person but once you got to know them you wanted nothing more to do with them? It is much like personality vs character. Some people have great exuberant, outgoing, friendly personalities. But once you get to know their character...adios!

Ladies, the Bible says that a quiet and gentle spirit will win over external adornment every time. I fell in love with Liz because I liked the way I felt when I was with her. Was I attracted to her beauty, sure I was. But as we mature in life together, it's the relationship that we have built through years of marriage that has stood the test of time. Do you realize how much pressure that takes off of both of you? To walk in confidence knowing that you can grow old gracefully together without fear of being traded in like a used car because you don't look the same as you did when you first got married or things have changed sexually. Going back to honoring your husband, it is so powerful to know that God can change him without you nagging or even saying a word. That's the power of honor coupled with prayer.

"...[A]s he observes your chaste and respectful behavior." Honor and respect is what makes you more attractive to your husband, it is more important than your physical beauty. Your outward appearance will change with age, but honor and respect can be with you always.

When God instructs you to honor your husband, he's not placing you in a subservient position, degrading you or making you a second-class citizen. He's bringing you into God's order of things and giving you the keys to your husband's heart. You'll never relate to any man properly without respect. I once observed a distant family member who, from the beginning of their relationship, disrespected her husband both privately and publicly. It was her way or the highway. The result of her disrespecting her own husband was that she disrespects all men. This couple is still together after many years, but it is obvious that he has been conditioned to take a subservient position in the relationship, and it is sad. The old adage, "Oh, we know who wears the pants in that relationship" may get some laughs, but in reality, it is a serious setback and out of sync with how God created us. Unfortunately, a wife usurping over her husband is a somewhat common trait with women who have suffered abandonment, cruelty or molestation by a male sometime in their lives. Without intervention and prayer, they may struggle throughout their entire lives with disdain, a lack of trust, and sometimes a disrespect of all men. Victims of such a tragic past may cause them to choose for a mate a man who releases leadership to them and allows themselves to be almost pushed around and controlled by his wife. Again, sad to see. Let's get back to respect. This principle of respect is even true with raising boys. They are basically little men. They need honor and affirmation in order to bring the best out of them. Stop screaming and yelling at them. Use authority, not volume.

Men (it's your turn now), the Number *one* need of a woman is *security*. You know the Bible has twice as much to say to the men as it does the women in regards to relational responsibility. Men, you're supposed to be a Christ-like example to your wife in order to cultivate the security that is so very important to her health and well-being. What makes women secure? 1) selflessness and sacrifice. In the early years of my marriage I didn't get this. I thought that she was here to meet all my needs. I was selfish, insensitive, un-sacrificial... Don't get me wrong, I worked hard, provided for the family, but was still very self-centered. I instigated insecurity in my wife until I changed my attitude. When a wife knows that she and the kids are #1 to her husband, it brings out the best in them. The Bible clearly teaches that men need to be nourishing, cherishing, laying our lives down and preferring her over their own "needs." Women feel secure when they have a selfless, sacrificial husband tuned into them (because that's what "intimacy" really is). Woman feel insecure when they are married to a selfish, detached man who is not in tune with them.

So, in short, what makes a man attractive to a woman is his sacrificial nature. Let me prove this through research: There have been studies and surveys with wives who have been asked "what makes your husband more sexually attractive to you?" This exact question was asked in numerous studies. Answer: In almost every case either on top of the list or in the top 3 was this response by women: "He is more sexually attractive to me... (Listen carefully guys. I'm about to give you more sex in your marriage.), ... when he works hard for me and the children and helps around the house."

In almost every study, this is basically the answer given. It's not how he dresses, styles his hair, the car he drives, the way he speaks... Nope, it's when we are not lazy and help with projects around the house. That is her place, her palace, her security. You know, I'm a bit concerned about men who spend more time than women getting ready for an outing. Hair, cologne, bling, GQ clothes, dying their hair, plucking eye brows, and yes...in some cases, even putting on a little make-up. Men seem to be more caught up with style and flair than character, self-sacrifice and integrity. Seems nowadays that men want to look pretty and women want to work. Oh, oh, some of you are getting angry with me about now. Well, there was another study that's been replicated over and over. The University of Pennsylvania actually did a study on the effects of male perspiration on women. That's right! These researches blindfolded women and applied male sweat on their upper lips. Now they didn't tell the women what it was, they just said it was a household product. Because if women knew what they were doing they would probably run out of that place. They applied the sweat and connected them to specialized machines that can detect physiological changes in the women. Guess what they found out.

When women were "under the influence (for lack of a better term)" of male sweat, they relaxed, they got happier and (here it is) it affected their menstrual cycle, and they even got aroused. How amazing is that! If you don't believe it, look it up on the internet. Does God know what he's doing when he says, "Men, sacrifice, work, serve her, work for her from the sweat of your brow...and you'll have a better marriage (sex life)." A lazy guy might say, 'I just want a wife that's always sexual and doesn't need all that...' They don't exist! Not in the real world anyway. So, when a husband serves, works, and sweats, the wife becomes affected in a way that gratifies both sides. Now, here is the interpretation of that study about the effects of sweat in relation to working around the house. Men, you may be just *one* house cleaning away from the height of your dreams.

Intimacy is the prize of marriage. If you have intimacy, you have everything. That's right. Real intimacy brings security for the woman and honor to the man. You cannot experience intimacy until two people open their hearts to one another. And you will never open your heart to a person who is threatening your most sensitive issues. Often, the unspoken message is this:

For a man: 'if you are dishonoring me, I will not open the door of my heart to you, it hurts too much.' For a woman: 'I'm not going to open the door and have you walk away and not care for me and not be tuned into me or be there when I need you.'

True intimacy in marriage = trust. The bottom line: a man trusts an honoring woman and a woman trusts a sacrificial man.

1) Act lovingly toward each other.
2) Treat each other with respect.
3) Give each other dignity.
4) Don't be overly concerned just about your own rights.
5) Do not curse at our spouse - under any circumstances.

Your words should build your spouse up, not tear him or her down.

A gentle answer turns away wrath, but a harsh word
stirs up anger.
- Proverbs 15:1

"Do not let any unwholesome talk come out of your mouths, but only what is helpful for building others up according to their needs, that it may benefit those who listen."

- Ephesians 4:29

How can we make our marriage work better?

Element #2
Develop Good Communication Skills

I always open each pre-marriage coaching session with an important principle. Progress will never be made in any relationship without open, honest reliable communication (remember OHRC?). The Bible tells us that

"Reliable communication permits progress"
- Proverbs 13:17

If this level of communication is not achieved and practiced, trouble is not far off. I love this quote: "Much unhappiness has come into the world because of bewilderment and things left unsaid." Open honest reliable communication is the only street that leads us into the real world. It allows a couple to grow together and blend as never before. Once we are on this road, happiness is on the horizon. I tell each couple that I counsel that the one hour we spend together each week will be in vain if they are not open and honest, and that nothing significant can be built on lies or deception, only on truth. But be patient.

Good communication is an acquired skill that takes time and effort to become polished in. You can talk with someone for years, every day, and it still won't mean much unless time is spent on deep conversation concerning what makes each other tick. Your likes, dislikes, concerns and frustrations must be discussed on a fairly regular basis in order to experience progress in the relationship. All too often what we try to communicate gets lost in translation despite our best intentions. We say one thing, the other person hears something else, and misunderstandings, frustration, and conflicts ensue. In order to mature (and not just get old), open, honest reliable communication is vital.

A recent poll revealed that the average couple only talks to each other together, alone for four minutes a day. Four minutes! In fact, according the *New York Daily News* (2012), Americans spend 34 hours a week watching TV, and DVR use has doubled in the past few years. 34 hours of TV and only 23 minutes talking alone together in a typical week. Again, you can't make any progress if you don't talk to each other. One of the reasons we have problems in communication is because men and women communicate differently. One of the major reason you have communication problems is you expect your mate to think like you do, and we don't. After over 40 years of marriage, we both still look at each in utter amazement after trying to communicate a point. Think of what you think, then think of the opposite and that's what they think.

Communication is about more than just exchanging information. It's about understanding the emotion and intentions behind the information. Effective communication is how you convey a message so that it is received and understood by someone in exactly the way you intended. Henry Winkler said, "Assumptions are the termites of relationships." More than just the words you use, effective communication combines a set of skills including attentive listening (constantly talking isn't necessarily communicating), managing stress in the moment, and the capacity to recognize and understand your own emotions and those of your spouse. Effective communication is the glue that helps you deepen your connections to others and improve teamwork, decision-making, and problem solving. It enables you to communicate even negative or difficult messages without creating conflict or damaging trust. Trust is so very important. It takes time to build but can be damaged or destroyed in a single careless moment. The more effort and practice you put into polishing your communication skills, the more it begins to flow and become part of who you are.

Let's look at some Barriers to Good Communication:

1) Dominating the conversation by doing most of the talking and not listening to the other person's full comments or feelings
2) Being rude
3) Being one sided

4) Raising your voice to make your point
5) Using terms like "You always, I never, you'll never change, I didn't sign up for this..."
6) Out-of-control emotion
7) Not admitting mistakes or not being open to the possibility that you may have missed something.
8) Invalidating the other person's feelings comments, observations or complaints by saying: "That's dumb or you're wrong to feel that way" etc.
9) Lack of proper focus—focusing on the person rather than the problem makes things personal.
10) Negative body language.

"Show your love by being helpful to each other."
- Ephesians 4:2

Let's now look at some ways of improving communication skills.

1. Be a good listener.

Most people will define communication as talking and getting their point across. However, effective communication is more about listening than it is about talking. Listening well means not just understanding the words or the information being communicated, but also understanding how the speaker feels about what they're communicating. I have a good friend who is also a pastor, and he is one of the best listeners I have ever met. He stops everything he is doing, makes good eye contact, nods his head, and follows absolutely everything you say. Anytime you talk to this man, you have his full attention. He has been a great example to me and I often think about the way he makes me feel when I talk to him. The way he listens adds value to the life of the person who is sharing with him. I try to remind myself to be more like him when people are talking to me rather than allowing myself to be distracted. When you really listen, you make the other person feel valued, which can help build a stronger, deeper connection between you.

If your goal is to fully understand and connect with the other person, listening effectively will often come naturally. If it doesn't, try the following tips. The more you practice them, the more satisfying and rewarding your interactions with others will become.

Tips for effective listening:

1) Focus fully on your spouse and avoid one of the biggest distractions I know today—cell phones.

There is almost nothing more frustrating than trying to pour your heart out to someone who is multi-tasking (texting). My wife has caught me doing this and has repeatedly pointed out that the person who was talking to me directed their conversation to someone else in the group as I juggled with the phone and their conversation. I felt terrible. I have since made a point to stop being distracted and concentrate on giving the person my full attention. Good listening also means that when someone is talking to us we do not look around the room or at other people. Focus your full attention on the person talking to you.

2) Look People in the Eye.

Many people feel a bit uncomfortable about looking into others' eyes, but studies show that doing this conveys truth and honor. Eye contact can communicate confidence, assurance, and understanding. It also allows for a stronger connection and usually makes it easier to read emotions. It also gives the person you are communicating with a sense of importance and attention. If you can't make eye contact from time to time, it may even arouse suspicion. This doesn't mean you should initiate a staring contest. Just make sure to put your spouse at ease by looking at them eye to eye occasionally.

3.) Avoid interrupting or trying to redirect the conversation to your concerns.

Avoid doing so by saying something like, "If you think that's bad, let me tell you what happened to me." Listening is not the same as waiting for your turn to talk. You can't concentrate on what someone's saying if you're forming what you're going to say next. Often, the speaker can read your facial expressions and know that your mind's elsewhere or that you are anxious to share your story with them.

4) Be empathetic

Feel what it is your spouse is trying to convey. Whether or not you're able to fully relate, your compassion won't go unnoticed. Spend a moment putting yourself in their position, what's going through their head and what it must be like for them. This can help you connect with them. Even if you fall short in understanding their feelings or experience, your attempt to care and be compassionate will go a long way in making a connection with them. I remember well people who seemed to really care when I was going through a struggle or shared something that I felt was important to me.

5) Have an open mind.

Whatever is important to my wife must be important to me. Even if it is not my opinion or the way I feel, I must come into meetings with an open mind. *Great listeners know that every conversation they have isn't going to resolve a larger issue.* Still, it puts them one step closer to understanding the people they communicate with on a daily basis. Listening allows each person to understand the other's thoughts and heart on issues.

6) Show your interest in what's being said.

Nod occasionally, smile at the person, and make sure your posture is open and inviting. Encourage the speaker to continue with small verbal comments like "yes" or "uh-huh."

2. Think before you speak.

Even if you don't know everything you want to say and things have a way of developing as the conversation goes on, you should have a general idea. Take the time to be clear about the points you want to make before talking. Always be honest in your communication.

3. Avoid exaggeration.

"Exaggeration" is defined as "to magnify beyond the limits of truth; overstate; represent disproportionately. Opening phrases like "you never, you always…" should be avoided at all costs as it only infuriates the listener. Also avoid, "You're not hurt, what a joke. You're just being too sensitive." Once you start exaggerating, the person's focus shifts from whatever your point was, to anger and retaliation.

Instead of focusing on the issue, he/she is now thinking of a comeback to your statement(s).

4. Watch your volume and the tone of your voice.

Volume should never be misunderstood as having authority. If you start yelling and raising your voice, the environment shifts from communication to one of hostility. Your spouse will immediately assume a defensive posture and will look at the situation as just another argument.

5. Provide feedback.

If there seems to be a disconnect, reflect what has been said by paraphrasing. "What I'm hearing is," or "Sounds like you are saying," are great ways to reflect back. Don't simply repeat what the speaker has said verbatim, though. You'll sound insincere or unintelligent. Instead, express what the speaker's words mean to you. Ask questions to clarify certain points: "What do you mean when you say," or "Is this what you mean?"

"Wisdom shows itself in being considerate."
- James 3:17

According to James, a mark of being wise is being considerate. When I'm being considerate, I'm being wise.

Element #3
Master the Art of Compromise

"Love does not demand its own way"
- 1 Corinthians 13:5

The mark of genuine love and maturity is the ability to compromise. It's being unselfish and caring about the needs and desires of your spouse. Do you insist on always having your own way in your marriage? Nobody wants to be with someone who is all about "my way or the highway! Love it or leave it!" You can't get your way all the time. Marriage is all

43

about mastering the art of compromise. You and your spouse have different preferences on some things.

Realistically, you have at least three options:

1) You could stubbornly insist until you get your way.
2) You could passively surrender to all of your spouse's wishes.
3) Both of you could compromise.

One of the problems is having a false perception of compromise. To many, it sounds as if neither of you will get what you want! Be assured that compromise need not be a lose-lose proposition...not if you do it right. But before considering how to compromise, there are a few things you should know about this vital skill. First of all, compromise requires *teamwork*. Before marriage, you might have been accustomed to making unilateral decisions. Now things have changed, and both you and your spouse must put your marriage above your personal preferences. Rather than think of that as a drawback, consider the advantage. The ideas of two people combined can lead to a solution that is better than what each one could come up with alone. I constantly draw from my wife's opinion on things. After all, she approaches things differently than I do. She tends to lean toward compassion, forgiveness, and has answers that reflect this nature. Mine is usually more cut and dry. The answer to almost everything usually rests between these two natures. Compromise (as with good communication) *requires* an open mind.

You don't have to agree with everything your spouse says or believes, but you have to be honestly open to considering his or her position. If you find yourself sitting with your arms folded and shaking your head no (or just thinking it) when your spouse is trying to talk out a problem with you, your discussion will never get anywhere. *Compromise requires self-sacrifice*. That's what marriage should be about: give *and* take, not just take.

Start right. The tone in which a discussion begins is often the tone in which it ends. If you start with harsh words, the chances of reaching a peaceful compromise are slim. So follow the Bible's advice:

"Clothe yourselves with compassion, kindness, humility, mildness, and patience"

- Colossians 3:12

Such qualities will help you and your spouse avoid arguing and get down to the work of problem solving. Search for common ground. If your attempts at compromise only escalate into heated arguments, it may be that you and your spouse are focusing too much on where your views differ. Instead, pinpoint where they agree. Chances are, you will find that the aspects that you both feel strongest about are not really all that incompatible. Be willing to adjust your view. The Bible says:

"Each one of you must love his wife as he does himself; on the other hand, the wife should have deep respect for her husband"

- Ephesians 5:33

When love and respect flow freely, both spouses are willing to consider the other's viewpoint, and even be swayed. This is the fruit of compromise. I made a list of some of the things that usually require compromise in a marriage.

1. How you spend your vacations

In planning the vacation, how much money should we spend? Do we visit several places, or go to one place? What arrangements need to be made in advance (pre-planning)? Chances are each of you have different ideas, and that's OK. However, you may need to compromise a bit. One year you take one person's kind of vacation, the next year you take the other person's kind. There's a give and take.

2. How your kids are raised

Discipline is a big one. Most married couples have slightly different ideas on how to discipline the children. Generally speaking, mom will tend to be much easier than Dad when it comes to discipline. One wants to talk, the other wants to spank. A good rule of thumb is always make the punishment fit the crime and remember to bring clear understanding to your child as to why you are disciplining them and what your expectancy is for change.

3. How your money is spent

One of the top five reasons for divorce is financial pressure and differences in how money is spent. Regular sit-down meetings with each other are needed for budgeting and financial planning. Prioritizing is the name of the game along with fairness in meeting each other's wants and expectations.

4. How often you make love and even the best time to make love

When it comes to sex, one of you is saying, "Drop everything" the other is saying, "Drop dead!" Some of you are naturally morning people—you're up and ready to go, including your hormones. Others are night owls—you don't believe in God before 11 a.m. in the morning, but at midnight, you're still going strong. Pre-planning and compromise are important in this area of marriage as well.

5. How often you see the in-laws

Empathy is crucial when it comes to planning visits to the in-laws. In many cases, one can be a little resistant depending on the relationship between a spouse and his/her in-laws. Remember that your in-laws are the loving parents of your spouse, and occasional visits are important your spouse.

6. How you spend your day off

It's not *your* day off anymore; it's the *family's* day off. Once you're married, it's no longer what *I* want to do on *my* day off, it's what *we* are going to do on *our* day off.

In all of the areas above, Compromise is crucial. It is a fact that more marriages die today from inflexibility (an unwillingness to bend or change) than from alcoholism, abuse, or adultery.

Element #4
Maintain Romance

Romance, physical affection, sex, fun, playfulness, and having time to enjoy each other must become part of your weekly routine. Too often this area is neglected, especially after having been married a few years. God intended for your marriage to be exciting and satisfying.

"...May you always be captivated by her love"
- Proverbs 5:19b, NLT

Notice that He says *"always."* Always in love, always charmed and fascinated by her love. You are to keep the courting going strong in your marriage. Rick Warren said, "If there was more courting in marriages, they'd be fewer marriages in court." The problem is that the things you did to win your mate's love, you've stopped doing. You've got to keep on *dating* your mate. Do you guys remember when you were dating your wife? I don't know about you but I brought flowers, wrote poems, had long phone conversations, looked and smelled my best, did things she wanted to do, watched movies that she chose for us... I romanced Liz! No matter how far along you find yourself in your relationship, you have to re-visit the dating days. Sometimes men can be pretty naive about the needs of our wives. We sometimes just don't get it.

A man went to a psychiatrist with his wife. He said, "My wife is depressed. I'm really concerned." The psychiatrist said, "Could I talk to her privately?" Psychiatrist talks to the woman and finds she is just starving for affection. He brings her man back into the room and to model it, the psychiatrist walks over to the man's wife, gives her a big hug and a big juicy kiss. He said, "She needs this every day of the week." The husband said, "I think I can only get her here Mondays, Wednesdays and Fridays. . ." Us guys can be kind of dumb. We need to make *our relationship* a priority.

Become best friends. Have fun. You need to develop common interests. For me and Liz, ministry has been our common denominator. We serve God together, so we are constantly sharing thoughts, reading the same type of books, and sharing our passion for the gospel. Are we different? Absolutely! That's what keeps it all so interesting and adventuresome. We also know what makes each other tick and still enjoy doing things together. For the vast majority of married couples that work separate jobs and have different hobbies and interests, a greater effort must be made to involve yourself in what the other person is involved in and interested in. If you don't, you run a high risk of experiencing separation rather than unity. We will cover this subject more thoroughly in chapter 9 (intimacy).

Element #5
Focus on Changing Yourself

I have come to realize that you *can't* change people. You can correct, offer constructive criticism, and encourage, but change comes through an individual, by an individual. All the nagging and hostility pointed toward a person's faults will not change them. The only person you have the power to change is you. In the vast majority of marriages, even if just one person follows these guidelines, the marriage will get better. Don't say, "I'll try if my mate tries." And don't focus on your mate's shortcomings. Instead, put your major effort into becoming the best husband or wife you can be. My character should never be contingent upon anyone else! Focus on changing *you*!

> Why do you look at the speck of sawdust in your brother's eye and pay no attention to the plank in your own eye? How can you say to your brother, "Let me take the speck out of your eye," when all the time there is a plank in your own eye? You hypocrite, first take the plank out of your own eye, and then you will see clearly to remove the speck from your brother's eye.
>
> - Matthew 7:3-5

Do you allow challenges in your marriage to change you for good? Do you focus on changing your spouse or changing yourself? Start by doing something every day that will bless your spouse and strengthen your marriage. This will get the focus off of all the things you think you need, and places the emphasis on loving your spouse. You will always bring the best out of your spouse when you place his or her needs above your own. Give this your best effort and you will reap the fruit of your labor.

> Whatever you do, work at it with all your heart, as working for the Lord, not for men.
>
> - Colossians 3:23

48

"Show your love by being helpful to each other"
- Ephesians 4:2

Ask your mate what is important to him or her (believe me, they'll tell you), and then put effort into these areas. I like to remind myself: "If it's important to her, it must become important to you." Don't take your marriage for granted. Be conscious of the fact that you will be judged by what you do, not what someone else does or doesn't do for you. I have talked into the lives of many struggling married couples about this. Many couples are living in a constant state of a "Mexican Stand Off." One is waiting for the other to change before they change themselves. Marriage is a divine work of art. God created it. First thing God did after creating Adam was to establish marriage. Who knows the book better than its author, and who knows the creature better than its Creator?

Allow God to use His brush! Becoming a masterpiece is about yielding to the artist. We are God's canvas, but we must allow Him to do His work in and through us. Remember that for every finger pointed at someone else, there are three pointing back to you. Enhance your marriage by changing yourself first, then pray for your spouse rather than pointing fingers and accusing. Praying together is the most important thing you can do for your marriage.

"Unless the LORD builds the house, its builders labor in vain. Unless the LORD watches over the city, the watchmen stand guard in vain."
- Psalm 127:1

Remember what love is and is not.

"Love does not demand its own way"
- 1 Corinthians 13:5

Element #6
Build a Solid Relationship with Christ

This is what will give you the *power* to do all those things. Jesus Christ gives you the power and ability to do the other things when human love wears out. I love what my pastor, Pastor Mike Neville taught me: *"Jesus gives you the ability to go*

49

beyond your own ability. That is the anointing!" Memorizing and believing this quote has always led me to look to the Lord for the power to say and do those things that would ordinarily be difficult for me on my own strength.

"Let this mind be in you which was also in Christ Jesus"

- Philippians 2:5

When you've got a husband and a wife both moving toward Christ, it brings you together. Nothing will bring your marriage closer than when you both focus on Christ. When you move toward Him, it automatically brings you together in spite of all your differences. Those of you who know me and Liz well, know that we are different in many areas except our commitment to Christ. She is spontaneous, I plan almost everything out. She is giddy and energetic, I tend to be more serious and subdued. But one thing has pulled us together, and has taught us to compromise and grow in all of these areas discussed. I'm a lot more like her than I was 40 years ago, and she's a lot more like me than she was 40 years ago because we learn from each other.

The greatest thing you can do for your marriage is put Jesus Christ right in the center of it. Then you start hanging out with other couples who are committed to making their marriages work by doing the same. Don't hang around couples that aren't committed to their marriage. I don't care how funny they are or how close they live to you. If they're not committed to their marriage, it's dangerous to have them as close friends. I'm serious! *Eighty-three percent* of all affairs occur between couples when one couple is not satisfied with their marriage. You should have as your closest friends those who are just as committed to saving their marriage as you are to saving yours. Find yourself a healthy church and find people just like that. Then read the Bible together and pray together and even memorize some scriptures together.

Please take time to pray this prayer:

Lord Jesus, help me to identify weaknesses in my life and my relationship with my spouse. I need your help (anointing) that transcends my own ability. Lord, help me to treat my spouse with love and respect regardless of the circumstances. I ask that you help us develop good communication skills. I confess that I struggle whenever compromise is needed. Help me to be creative in keeping the romance fire burning bright. I ask that you give me a good sense of humor and the ability to laugh more. Do I laugh enough? From this day on I am determined to concentrate on changing me and not my spouse.   Last but not least, I know that in order to see my life and marriage flourish, I need to build my relationship with You, Jesus Christ. I pray all of this in the name of my Lord and Savior Jesus Christ. Amen.

Chapter 4
Guns N' Roses - Resolving Conflict

ISN'T IT AMAZING how we can love our spouse so much yet at times almost hate them. These are stressful times in which we live. And almost every day you hear about another home where the string has snapped. The truth about marriages is that 10 out of 10 have struggles. But, just like anything else, we get what we put into it. If we truly work toward peace and start with ourselves, we can experience positive change and help make it a blessing instead of a bondage.

> When a man is gloomy, everything seems to go wrong; when he is cheerful, it's like a continual feast! Better is having little with the fear of the Lord, than great treasure with trouble. Better is a dinner of only herbs where love is, than a huge meal with hatred. An angry man stirs up strife, but he who is slow to anger decreases contention. Without counsel, plans go wrong, but in the multitude of counselors they are established.
>
> - Proverbs 15:15-18,22

You will notice that in this passage there are some negative words... *sorrow(v13), gloomy (v15), trouble (v16), hatred (v17), strife (v18), and wrong (v22).* These are all synonyms for *stress* and *tension.* They represent those times when the string gets too tight...and then it snaps! A guitar string can snap if too tight. The balloon seems fine, it can take a little more, then boom! A rubber band can be stretched only so far, then ouch! A volcano beneath surface...fire! Pressure cooker boils over! An old saying of mine is "A devil exposed, is a devil defeated."

So let's have a look at the "devils" (reasons), the response, and how to resolve conflicts in our marriage.

Why Does Conflict Exist?

If you're going to overcome conflict in your life, you have to understand why it is there. The Bible says,

"Where do you think all these appalling wars and quarrels come from? Do you think they just happen? Think again. They come about because you want your own way, and fight for it deep inside yourselves"
- James 4:1, Message

That's where most of our conflict comes from—because we want our own way. Statements like, "I want what I want, I never get…, you always…, I'm not getting what I want out of this relationship, I didn't sign up for this…" are all tell-tale signs of a one sided, self-centered relationship. Notice that the Bible tells us that conflict doesn't "just happen." They arise because we *want our own way and fight for it."* Clear, isn't it? The seed bed of conflict lies within us and we fight to keep it.

What is Your Reaction to Conflict?

As we look at these reactions, let me remind you of the verse in *Psalm 139:23* where David wrote, *"Search me, O God, and know my heart; try me, and know my anxieties.* "This is one of the keys to responding to marital conflict—looking at ME and how I am reacting to the situation. We tend to look for someone else to blame and fail to realize that for every finger pointed toward the other person, there are *three* pointing back to us. If we would only be open to the truth that there are always two sides to every story, and that we have more power than we think to reach deep within ourselves, we can do the right thing. Without fail, each time I find myself having a conflict with my wife, my response is worse than the offense. We overreact, we exaggerate, we point our fingers, we raise our voices, we bring up the past… and the list goes on and on. There is another thing I have learned through the years: nobody makes me do anything.

How many times have we heard phrases like, "*She* made me punch the wall, or *he* made me scream…" I will cover the subject of anger in the next chapter, but let me say that nobody "makes" you do anything you don't want to do. Our reaction to any conflict is on us! It's nobody else's fault. they don't make us do things, we do what we do out of a lack of control and restraint. If you are a praying person, you have access to the greatest power in the universe—God. The Bible says, "the reason you don't have what you need is because you don't ask." Ask God for help, ask for strength, grace, and revelation. Ask God to show you the reason why you react the way you do when angry or upset. Get ready. Chances are, the Holy Spirit will take you on a journey of your past. A place and reference point to show you why you react the way you do.

How Do We Resolve Conflict?

This is a tough question to answer completely in its entirety. There probably is no one answer. However, I know for sure that if we apply ourselves and keep the principles of this chapter in our minds and hearts, we can resolve most of our conflicts. We have learned that the reason for conflict is that "we want things *our own way,*" the origin of which is found "deep *within ourselves.*" This needs to be rooted out through:

1. An awareness that it is there.

Alcoholics Anonymous tells new members of their discussion groups, "If you confess you have a problem with alcohol you are well on your way to recovery." We must admit that there is a problem before we begin our recovery.

2. A desire to have it removed.

Once you get to a point that you really are sick and tired of fighting and arguing, going to sleep with an imaginary line drawn across the middle of your bed, silent treatments, etc., then you're ready to resolve things.

3. Prayer.

Prayer is said to be the key to heaven. Prayer is talking to your creator who knows everything about everything, including your problems. I don't know how many conflicts have been resolved in our marriage by simply stopping to pray together about the situation. Do war on the floor (prayer), not in the air (argument). Through prayer, you are not praying about your point or against your spouse's point, but for overall peace in your marriage. Liz is usually the one who initiates this approach but how can I say "No" to allowing God to speak wisdom into our madness? Did you know that you can pray out what pastors usually have to counsel out? We all need to learn to ventilate *vertically*. You will find that prayer is not only therapeutic, but is also one of the greatest weapons we can access in the war against the battles that wage within us.

4. Your willingness to put your head on the chopping block and ask your spouse how you are doing in your recovery.

It is important to develop a system that allows coming together and praying for the relationship. Preventive maintenance will usually save you from a breakdown. Try to catch yourself before things escalate, and initiate on the *spot prayer*. Yes, that's right, pray with each other before things get too far out of hand. I admit, this is sometimes easier said than done, but developing the habit of coming to God and praying for peace in the middle of your muddle will turn things around. Food for thought: as you talk to God about the problems you're facing, you may discover that the problem is a need that only God can meet. Many times, we become frustrated at our spouse because they are failing to meet a need that *we think* they should be meeting. *The truth is that we should not expect people to meet needs in our lives that only God can meet.*

Back in chapter 2, I shared a quote by Ruth Graham that I believe is worth repeating: "I pity the married couple who expect too much from one another. It's foolish to expect from one another that which Jesus Christ can be—always ready to forgive, totally understanding, unendingly patient, invariably tender and loving, unfailing in every area, anticipating every need, making more than adequate provision. Such expectations put a marriage under an impossible strain." When you find yourself constantly angry with another person, ask yourself, "Am I asking them to do things that only God can do? Am I asking a human to be God?" What a huge mistake it is to think that your spouse is going to be a perfect mate. No way. So, allow his/her humanity and look to God as the source of your strength, encouragement, peace, power, forgiveness, love etc. You will find that He and only He can meet all of those needs.

If and when you do find yourself in a conflict, remember that even countries have limitations on what weapons can or cannot be used. Here are my suggestions to the rules of engagement in times of a war:

The Eleven Rules of Engagement

Rule of Engagement #1: Never bring up the other person's family to prove a point.

This will only cause further problems, stir up anger which will most likely result in resentment. If bitter exchanges take place using phrases like, "You're just like so-and-so," "You got that from your mother," "The acorn doesn't fall far from the tree, you and your family…," get ready to repair some deeply rooted hurts caused by your statements.

Rule of Engagement #2: Go after the issue, not each other.

Friendly fighting sticks with the *issue*. Neither party resorts to name-calling, cursing or character assassination. It's enough to deal with the problem without adding the new problem of hurting each other's feelings.

Rule of Engagement #3: Listen respectfully.

When people feel strongly about something, it's only fair to hear them out. Respectful listening means acknowledging their feelings, either verbally or through focused attention. It means never telling someone that he or she "shouldn't" feel that way (it *trivializes* their trauma). It means *saving* your point of view until after you've let the other person know you acknowledge how they feel about the subject, even if you don't fully comprehend.

Rule of Engagement #4: Talk softly.

QUOTE: "Some people think that you have to be the loudest voice in the room to make a difference. That is just not true. Often, the best thing we can do is turn down the volume. When the sound is quieter, you can actually hear what someone else is saying. And that can make a world of difference." - Nikki Haley

Rule of Engagement #5: Get curious, not defensive.

Both getting too defensive about yourself, and turning the tables to attack, escalate the fight. Instead, ask for more information, details, and examples. There is usually some basis for the other person's complaint. When you meet a complaint with curiosity, you make room for understanding. Choosing to take the high road by seeking more information for clarity, rather than immediately raising a defense guard, communicates to your spouse that you are giving him/her the benefit of the doubt. You are also affirming that your spouse is capable of reason and that his/her discontentment about a situation is valid, or at the very least you are reassuring them that they are not being "unreasonable," "petty," or "babyish"

That, through years of living together, they have proven to you that they are sensible people, and for them to be so upset about something, there must be a good reason/ misunderstanding.

That initial benefit of the doubt displays humility that perhaps you were wrong, but also communicates your love and trust in your spouse to be reasonable in their display of discontentment. Benefit of the doubt = "my spouse loves and trusts my better judgment/discretion"

Rule of Engagement #6: Ask for specifics.

Statements that include the words "always" and "never" almost *always* get you nowhere and are *never* true. When your partner has complaints, gently ask for specific examples so that you can have a clear understanding of what he or she is talking about. When you have complaints, do your best to give your partner examples to work with.

Rule of Engagement #7: Find points of agreement.

In almost every conflict, there can be found some points of agreement. Finding common ground, even if it's a simple agreement that there is a disagreement or problem, is an important start to finding a common solution.

Rule of Engagement #8: Look for options.

Fighting ends when cooperation begins. Asking politely for suggestions or alternatives invites collaboration. Consideration of options, especially those offered by your spouse, shows respect. Offering alternatives of your own shows that you also are willing to try something new.

Rule of Engagement #9: Compromise.

Sometimes, all it takes is small concessions to turn the situation around. If you give a little, it makes room for the other person to compromise too. Compromise doesn't have to mean that you're meeting each other exactly 50-50. Sometimes it's a 60:40 or even an 80:20 agreement. This isn't about scorekeeping. It's about finding a solution that is workable for both of you.

Rule of Engagement #10: Make peace.

Liz and I have agreed that our relationship is more important than winning arguments. Sometimes this meant we stayed up late until we came to a workable compromise.
The overall desire deep within every human being is to live in peace. Whenever peace seems impossible, remember and access the Prince of Peace (Jesus!).

Rule of Engagement #11: Pray together as soon as possible.

You're probably thinking about how difficult it may be to pray after a heated discussion. Chances are, one of you is naturally more apt to forgive quicker than the other. The quick forgiver usually doesn't like conflict to linger and attempts to make peace almost immediately (my wife). The other (me) tends to continue to analyze and hold on to a grudge over a longer period of time, usually too long. The real challenge is for both of you to agree as part of preventive maintenance that you will both do all that you can to come together after a conflict in prayer *in spite of your feelings*. This is a discipline to be sure, but critically important for both to come to a place of *dependence* on God for resolution and ultimately healing. Prayer has the amazing capacity to have us look to God, and acquire humility and compassion.
After all, looking to God should remind us of our own faults and failures, thus producing a sense of humility.

Whenever you remember how much grace God has bestowed upon you, the easier it is to forgive the other person you find yourself in conflict with. Remember the overall goal in any healthy relationship: to work together and enjoy life. Pray together after every conflict ("…pray without ceasing…").

"A home filled with strife and division destroys itself"
- Mark 3:25, TLB

The real danger with conflict is this: too much conflict can kill a marriage. We know that conflicts are bound to rise in any situations, which is why we need to get ready for it. That's what this chapter is all about. We're going to take a look at what the Bible has to say on how we understand conflict and resolve it in our lives. There are principles that we're going to focus on that will help you navigate through marital conflict as well as any other relationships. If you're single, you can obviously use these with your kids, friends, or colleagues at work, because all relationships are subject to conflict.

Anger Management

How can we end a discussion on resoling conflict without mentioning anger? What does it take to set you off? Before dealing with the important subject of anger management, allow me to inject a bit of anger humor:

Andy
Andy came to work one day, limping something awful. One of his co-workers, Josh, noticed and asked Andy what happened. Andy replied, "Oh, nothing. It's just an old hockey injury that acts up once in a while." Josh, "Wow, I never knew you played hockey." Andy, "No I don't. I hurt it last year when I lost $100 on the Stanley Cup Play-Offs. I put my foot through the television."

Glenn
After spending 31/2 hours enduring long lines, rude clerks and insane regulations at the Department of Motor Vehicles, Glenn Vaughan stopped at a toy store to pick up a gift for his son. "I brought my selection— a baseball bat—to the cash register," he said. "Cash or

charge?" the clerk asked. "Cash," he snapped. Then apologizing for his rudeness, he explained, "I've spent the entire afternoon at the DMV." The woman sweetly replied, "Shall I gift-wrap the bat...or are you going back there?"

Have you ever heard the expression, "It's enough to make a preacher cuss"? It reminds me of the story about a little boy trying to sell a lawn mower. The local pastor walked up and he was able to persuade him to buy the worn-out lawn mower. The pastor pulled on the rope several times to make sure the mower would start, but nothing happened. Not even a spit or a sputter. The boy told the preacher that he would have to kick the mower and say a few cuss words before the mower would crank. The preacher said, "Son, I can't do that. It's been years since I said a cuss word." The little boy replied, "Just keep pulling and it will come back to you."

According to an article I recently read, an estimated 1 in 5 Americans has issues with uncontrolled anger. 28% of homicides start with a domestic dispute in the home, and only 7% were gang-related! How do you keep anger from exploding into sin? The answer is in the Bible:

And "don't sin by letting anger control you." Don't let the sun go down while you are still angry, for anger gives a foothold to the devil
- Ephesians 4:26,27, NLT

Can you think of a time/times when your anger got the best of you? Can you remember a time when your anger got you in trouble or led to sin? How do you keep anger from exploding into sin? First of all, don't allow it to control you! As scripture warns us, "Don't ever go to bed harboring anger in your heart (don't carry anger into the next day)." Why not? Because anger gives the Devil a "foothold."

Five Ways to Control Your Anger

1. Don't waste too much time and energy on petty disagreements.

Sensible people control their temper; they earn respect by overlooking wrongs.

- Proverbs 19:11, NLT

Marital maturity is all about overlooking wrongs. If you have been married for any length of time (post-honeymoon), you will begin to notice things about your spouse that get under your skin. Some of them are things that come up as a result of cultural differences. Everyone is raised differently and has developed traits, habits, and things that may seem strange to someone raised differently. Take it from me most of these traits never go away; you just have to learn to overlook them. Liz was raised in a much different environment than I was. Does this cause problems sometimes? Sure, it does. But through the years, we have acquired the ability to sidestep, overlook, or compensate for those differences. As a matter of fact, the differences that used to create conflict have now become fun or funny. The things that used to cause anger, we now make provisions for.

Let me give you an example or two. Liz misplaces her house keys, car keys, and cell phone on a regular basis, and there has been no change in 40 years of marriage. Sometimes she will yell out "Honey, call my cell phone please", several times a day, and the search begins. Because Liz usually has her phone in the vibrate mode, we pause silently in different parts of the house, listening intently for the slight vibration sound. What had once been a nuisance has now become a family activity that we participate in all seriousness whenever the occasion rises. Well, I used to lecture her, raise my voice, explain the importance of keeping track of things, discuss safety issues associated with having your keys when you need them etc. etc. etc. Then all of sudden, something dawned on me: the keys are not at the top of her priority list, and isn't worth causing a fuss over. After all, it is inevitable.

So, instead of fighting about it all the time, I decided to make spare keys and strategically place them on the key ring in the kitchen, taped under her car bumper and placed in her purse. As far as her cell phone is concerned, thank God for technology! I recently purchased a small device that allows you to trace your lost keys or cell phone by a push of a button. It sounds a tune when activated. Hallelujah! There's still a catch: one must *find* the keys to push the button or use the cell phone feature to locate your misplaced keys. Well, we've solved most of the problem.

Of course, it works both ways. During the course of my marriage Liz has tried to get me to stop throwing my clothes on the floor next to my side of the bed. She works very hard to keep everything nice and clean in the house, and no matter how many times she tells me about it, I always seem to defer back to my old habit. What did she do after years and years of trying to get me to change my evil ways? She placed a basket on the floor next to my bed where I can put my clothes in. It hasn't really changed me, but she provided a way to satisfy both of us without resorting to continued lectures or anger. Anyway, it is my summation that mannerisms and expression change from person to person. Getting angry about differences isn't worth it. *"A fool gives vent to anger, a wise man keeps control."* Can you identify with this? Have you ever done something in anger that made a fool of you? Anger and sin go hand in hand.

"An angry man stirs up dissension (friction/conflict), and a hot-tempered one commits many sins"
- Proverbs 29:22

Remember, our jails and prisons are full of people who could not control their anger just for this critical few moments. Think of almost every violent crime committed, most of those acts are rooted in anger. I still remember the words of my mother any time I would get upset: "Count to 10."

"…a quick-tempered man does foolish things…"
- Proverbs 14:17a

Here's a great quote by Seneca: "One of the greatest remedies for anger is delay." Road rage is a term that surfaced just the past two decades or so. Too many angry, frustrated, out of control people are out there on the road. One man cited for speeding said, "Well, I have a guardian angel on my bumper." His friend answered, "Yes, but those angels jump off the bumpers after 55 mph." When you let anger get the best of a situation you find yourself in situations where you tie the hands of God from interceding on your behalf! When you take things into your own hands, it takes the place of whatever God may want to do. Want to know what else anger does? It almost always distorts the truth! Anger can cause you to see things that aren't really there (so does jealousy). Remember, Satan is the *father of lies*. We not only see things that aren't really there, but it is much easier to perceive things differently from what they really are. Have you ever been upset or angry at someone and said, "I don't care what you say, I know what you were thinking." Hmm, and I thought that was a power only God had. Anger makes mountains out of ant-hills. Anger clouds your mind, causes you to lose the ability to make rational judgments. *"A person without self-control is like a city with broken-down walls."* Another translation of the Bible puts it this way:

"A person who cannot control himself is like a city with no walls."
- Proverbs 25:28

Anything can come in! Another good remedy for out of control anger is love!

"Love is not easily angered...[and] keeps no record."
- I Corinthians 13:4-5, NIV

I still love singing the song, "More love, more power, more of Jesus in my life..."
After each point, I invite you to take "the anger test." On a scale of 1 to 10, how well do you take control of your anger? Are you able to ignore petty disagreements? Are you patient and calm, or do you often reach points where you lose control? Grade yourself accordingly and keep in mind you may want to *share* your evaluation with your spouse and see if they agree.

1   2   3   4   5   6   7   8   9   10

2. Avoid close associations with other people prone to anger.

Make no friendship with an angry man, and with a furious man do not go lest you learn his ways and set a snare for your soul.
- Proverbs 22:24,25, NKJV

They say "If you lie with dogs, you'll get up with fleas." You become who you hang around with. If you hang around people who carry an angry spirit, it will eventually rub off on you. According to the scripture we just read, it will even lead to your demise (snare/trap of your soul)! Right about now you're probably thinking, 'Great, what do you do when your married to an angry person? If you live with a person who carries this anger with them, you can't totally ignore them, but you can develop a strong prayer life that protects you from slipping into that spirit. I highly recommend praying over each part of the home and being mindful of the potential of his/her influence upon your life. Don't become like the woman who was bitten by a rabid dog, was on the verge of death from rabies. The doctor told her to put her final affairs in order. So, the woman took pen and paper, and began writing furiously.

In fact, she wrote and wrote and wrote. Finally, the doctor said, "That sure is a long will you're making." She snorted, "Will, nothing! I'm making a list of all the people I'm going to bite before I die!" In short, choose your friends wisely and make sure that you surround yourself with positive people. Start by choosing friends who celebrate others and not simply tolerate them.

On a scale of 1-10, where do you find yourself as far as what kind of people you surround yourself with? Are they prone to negativity and anger? Evaluate yourself on how carefully you choose your friends.

1   2   3   4   5   6   7   8   9   10

3. Respond with an appropriate answer.

> A soft answer turns away wrath, but a harsh word stirs up anger.
>
> > - Proverbs 15:1

Whatever begins in anger usually ends in shame. The trick is to experience anger, but not allow it to drive you to say and do things that you will regret later. The scripture is crystal clear and so true. Problems escalate as we engage in mudslinging and a harsh exchange of words. It will amaze you how much can be defused by not responding to anger with anger, and choosing to respond with words of wisdom and kindness instead. Cursing catapults the situation into rage. Do you avoid conflict by using soft speech, or do you jump into the madness by engaging in vile conversation?

On a scale of 1-10, how well do you respond to attacks?

1   2   3   4   5   6   7   8   9   10

4. Communicate truthfully and honestly so anger doesn't build up.

I know we covered this subject in the "communication" chapter. OHRC—open, honest, reliable communication—produces success. *Wounds from a sincere friend are better than many kisses from an enemy (Proverbs 27:6 (NLT))*. The old song, "smiling faces tell lies" can be true in many cases. Most people won't really tell you the truth about you. There is a whole list of reasons this is true, but this is not what we need. The thing we really need to hear is an honest assessment from a friend (even when it hurts to hear it). If I have a cavity and visit the dentist, I need the truth and an honest assessment! Don't tell me I'm fine only to have my tooth fall out later at work. Even though the truth may hurt a bit, it leads to self-evaluation, and eventually deliverance and healing.

The other alternative is having a problem dealt with before it decays and infects. The keyword here is *honesty*. Receive constructive criticism rather than surrounding yourself with a bunch of people who are not willing to speak into your life. The one person in life who has the greatest impact when it comes to change is my own wife. Why? She can be brutally honest! She is the one who I can always count on to tell me the truth about myself. This brings me to one of two decisions: 1) ignore her and make excuses for myself; or 2) change! Quite frankly, at this point in my life, I would much rather hear the truth from a friend than kisses from an enemy.

How to turn a disagreement into a feud:

a.   Let your own feelings build up so you are in an explosive frame of mind.

b.   Assume you know all the facts, you are totally right and do most of the talking.

On a scale of 1-10, how honest are you when it comes to communicating. Do you communicate truthfully and kindly or let things brew inside of you to the point of explosion?

1   2   3   4   5   6   7   8   9   10

5. Stop thinking that you're all that!

> And why do you look at the speck in your brother's eye, but do not consider the plank in your own eye? Or how can you say to your brother, 'Let me remove the speck from your eye'; and look, a plank is in your own eye? Hypocrite!
>
> — Matthew 7:3-5

It's part of our fallen nature to point the finger at someone else rather than see that we too, have quirks and faults. Just because someone else's fault is different from ours doesn't give us the right to judge them. Remember: when you point your finger at someone, there are three more pointing back to you. Who died and made you the judge over everybody else? People aren't perfect—you're not perfect! How arrogant we can be sometimes. Who lied to you and told you that you were all that? Who lied and told you that you're better than everybody else, and have the right to point the finger at them? Hint: it wasn't God!

> He who is slow to anger is better than the mighty, and he who rules his spirit than he who takes a city.
>
> — Proverbs 16:32, NKJV

Pride comes before a fall but there is greatness in a person who is slow to anger and has control over oneself. The Bible teaches the we are to humble ourselves in the sight of the Lord, if we do, He will lift us up.

On a scale of 1-10, how do you honestly rate yourself in the area of humility, giving someone else the benefit of the doubt and not always getting your way in an argument/issue?

1   2   3   4   5   6   7   8   9   10

More Anger Management Tips

1. Be careful *what* you say and *how* you say it.

Be quick to hear, slow to speak, slow to anger resolve
anger before the sun goes down.

- James 1:19

Whether you want to lash out or bury your anger deep
inside, the instruction is to calm down and deal with problem
immediately. Things spoken hastily can hurt. Words are like a
shot arrow, powerful and cannot be taken back once they have
reached their destination. Think, listen and calm down before
you react. Then deal with anger *immediately*, not weeks, months
or even years later.

Here's a story about using the "silent treatment.": Mike and
Joan were having some problems at home, and were giving
each other the "silent treatment." But then Mike realized that
he would need his wife to wake him at 5:00 AM for an early
morning drive with some pals to a golf match. Not wanting to
be the first to break the silence (hence lose the "war"), he
wrote on a piece of paper, "Please wake me at 5:00 AM." The
next morning, Mike woke up, only to discover it was 9:00 AM
and that his friends would have left for the golf course without
him. Furious, he was about to go and see why his wife hadn't
awakened him when he noticed a piece of paper by the bed.
The paper said, "It is 5:00 AM. Wake up." Men simply are not
equipped for these kinds of contests.

2. Don't give full expression of your anger.

A fool vents all his feelings, but a wise man holds
them back

- Proverb 29:11

We may be angry, but none of us have the license to
unleash it on someone. Control your tongue and behavior.
Self-control is a fruit of the spirit. Cursing, hitting, breaking
things, and intimidating others are not godly behaviors.
Remember, our prisons are full of people who gave vent to
their anger for just a moment. The term used to describe such
an unleashing of anger is sometimes referred to as "temporary

insanity." Don't allow your anger to manifest in ways that you will regret afterwards. Research actually shows that when you express anger by screaming, yelling punching pillows, raging or throwing tantrums, you actually increase anger rather than reduce it contrary to popular belief, ventilation does not make anger go away

3. Don't get caught up in name calling and profanity.

> But I say, if you are even angry with someone, you are subject to judgment! If you call someone an idiot, you are in danger of being brought before the court. And if you curse someone, you are in danger of the fires of hell.
>
> - Matthew 5:22, NLT

This can't mean what it says! Or can it? Name-calling leading to Judgment, hell fire? Name-calling and bullying is not Christ-like behavior and have no more place in a marriage relationship than anywhere else. Not only are they damaging, but serve no purpose other than to hurt the other person. Because of the nature of marriage (two becoming one), it damages the other person as well as yourself.

> "All the utterances of my mouth are in righteousness; There is nothing crooked or perverted in them. They are all straightforward to him who understands, and right to those who find knowledge."
>
> - Proverbs 8:8,9, NASB

The scripture talks about speech that is fruitful and positive. What are the effects of profanity? Well, among other things, it breaks the spirit.

> Kind words bring life, but cruel words crush your spirit.
>
> - Proverbs 15:4, GNT

> Death and life are in the power of the tongue, and those who love it will eat its fruit. He who guards his mouth and his tongue, Guards his soul from troubles.
>
> - Proverbs 18:21,23

9 Things About the Power of Profanity

1. Profanity cripples our ability to say anything righteous.

If you cuss at work or home, it cripples your effectiveness to be a good witness to the goodness of God in your life. How can you effectively communicate the quality of life within you while cursing? The Bible tells us that bitter and sweet water should not come from the same fountain.

2. Profanity creates an atmosphere of hostility.

I recently counseled a married couple who resorts to cursing each other out when a dispute breaks out. The result is resentment, and an almost constant feeling of disrespect toward one another. Resentment is difficult to overcome. It takes a painstaking effort to overcome the ill-feelings that accompany bad language. Remember, there is a language that "breaks the spirit." Some words are indelible (the power of life and death is in the tongue). When we cuss, we're not dealing with a word or a sentence, but a spirit which takes a hold of those words and cuts deep. It is a spirit which ministers pain and hostility. Think about what we are really trying to accomplish when we curse at someone. Profanity is usually used to win an argument or intimidate the other person into a type of submission. This is never fruitful but damages the relationship.

3. Profanity substitutes God's boldness with an arrogant, brassy, and hostile attitude.

When it comes to our tongue (words we speak and language we use), there is no better reference than that of Book of James:

> For we all stumble in many ways. If anyone does not stumble in what he says, he is a perfect man (perfect meaning "complete"), able to bridle the whole body as well. Now if we put the bits into the horses' mouths so that they may obey us, we direct their entire body as well. Behold, the ships also, though they are so great and are driven by strong winds, are still directed by a very small rudder, wherever the inclination of the pilot

desires. So also the tongue is a small part of the body, and yet it boasts of great things. Behold, how great a forest is set aflame by such a small fire! And the tongue is a fire, the {very} world of iniquity; the tongue is set among our members as that which defiles the entire body, and sets on fire the course of our life, and is set on fire by hell. For every species of beasts and birds, of reptiles and creatures of the sea, is tamed, and has been tamed by the human race. But no one can tame the tongue; it is a restless evil and full of deadly poison. With it we bless our Lord and Father; and with it we curse men, who have been made in the likeness of God; from the same mouth come both blessing and cursing. My brethren, these things ought not to be this way. Does a fountain send out from the same opening both fresh and bitter water?

- James 3:2-11

James was talking about things that needed to be addressed. I believe that if you were to read these passages of scripture often, you will find deliverance from bad language and experience a breakthrough in your marriage (or any relationship for that matter). Think about your tongue as a rudder of a ship. The rudder determines whether or not the ship should stay on course. Here in James, the church needed this teaching despite all its beauty and power. People who loved God and wanted to serve Him were being ministered to. There is a flow of the Holy Spirit which will help us to keep pure and clean.

4. Profanity diminishes the creative power of the tongue.

Cursing destroys and inflicts injures. It is destructive rather than being constructive.

5. Profanity diverts the mind to the world's spirit.

6. Profanity sacrifices Godly character for personal acceptance.

And do not be conformed to this world, but be transformed by the renewing of your mind, that you may prove what is that good and acceptable and perfect will of God

- Romans 12:2

7. Profanity depends on shock to establish authority or create humor.

It indicates the decay of the human mind and can create terror or intimidation. It is often used to force others to conform to our way of thinking.

8. Profanity cheapens life's most precious relationships.

The people within the sphere of our influence are a gift from God and should always be valued. Family, friends, work associates, etc. are all people that have the capacity to add value to our lives and vice versa. "You're a..." Two of the most common profane phrases used today describes illegitimacy (bastard) and incest (alluding to family member(s) in inappropriate ways). What's happening is this culture, with the help of media, normalizes perversion, which is too often communicated through our words. The bible says perverse words breaks the spirit and crushes sensitivities towards the Holy Spirit.

9. Profanity erodes sensitivity toward eternal issues.

The horror of hell and the consequences of being damned is being neutralized. Because we say it so much nobody takes it really serious. Satan has normalized spiritual terms more than any other: "God damn, Hell" Is it accidental that these words are used so frequently?

We are tearing down the very people that we claim to love and want to spend the rest of our lives with. What shall we do? Confront yourself; commit to influencing others in a positive way. Raise your children properly. Teach them early what cuss words mean, and their destructive potentials. Confess it as sin and repent of it.

Spirits which could accompany a person using profanity include but aren't limited to:

1) Spirit of uncleanness
2) lust

3) hatred
4) anger
5) murder
6) death
7) blasphemy
8) anti-Christ

People use the name of Christ so much in the world that they don't see the name of Jesus as anything but a curse word. They see no redemptive power at all in a name which has been used and abused. *"Those who call upon the name of the Lord shall be delivered."*

A Few More Anger Management Tips

1. Be careful what you say and how you say it.

2. Don't give full expression of your anger.

3. Don't get caught up in name-calling and profanity.

4. Don't get back at/take revenge on an aggressor.

> Dear friends, never take revenge. Leave that to the righteous anger of God. For the Scriptures say, "I will take revenge; I will pay them back," says the Lord.
> - Romans 12:19, NLT

Here is another case where if we take things into our own hands (revenge) it ties up the hands of God on the matter: For we know the one who said, *"I will take revenge. I will pay them back."* He also said,

> "The Lord will judge his own people."
> - Hebrews 10:30, NLT

We live in a culture inundated with lawsuits and revenge. The Lord says vengeance is His and He will repay it. Admittedly, this isn't a popular position and very difficult to accept. Still, don't repay evil with evil. Marriages that build on revenge are headed for divorce.

Forgive those who anger you, forgive others as Christ has forgiven you

- Matthew 6:14

It doesn't matter how justified you are in your position, if your spouse is wrong, you are to forgive. After all, you didn't deserve Christ's forgiveness, but he gave it to you anyway. Do the same for your spouse.

5. Get to the *source* of your anger.

Search me, O God, and know my heart; test me and know my anxious thoughts. Point out anything in me that offends you and lead me along the path of everlasting life.

- Psalm 139:23,24, NLT

Search your heart and be honest. What are you really angry about, and who are you judging? Ask the tough questions so that you can effectively deal with the root of your anger. You may have to think and pray about the actual source of anger, because sometimes it isn't immediately evident. Often in therapy, couples will be angry with spouses about things in the past.

6. Don't stay angry.

But now is the time to get rid of anger, rage, malicious behavior, slander, and dirty language.

- Colossians 3:8

This is the key: feel angry, try to resolve the problem, and then *move on*. You can get physically and emotionally ill if you hang on to anger. Bitterness can develop and fester. Not everything in life is resolvable, so learn to *let go*. There have been several things over the course of my 40-year marriage that were not resolved to our 100% satisfaction; we both just decided to let it go and move on. You will find lots of little issues in your marriage that may cause disagreement, much of which will be worked out. Then there are some things we simply learn to live with. There it is again, my wife's voice whispering, "Don't sweat the small stuff Fern." This has proven to be a timeless advice.

7. Give the anger to God.

Cast your cares upon Him because He cares for you.
- 1 Peter 5:7

Ultimately, release anger to God; give it to Him. He tells us to cast all our cares upon Him. He can handle it and do more to heal us than any apology or revenge could ever accomplish.

8. Don't make excuses for your anger.

What you justify you buy. It's easy to say, "That's just the way I am" or "My father was like this and I learned it from him." *Take responsibility.* You are not a victim of people, circumstances, or even your environment. You are responsible for your own behavior no matter what.

9. Don't jump to conclusions.

Ask yourself, is my anger based on a real situation, or is my perception off? Sometimes we misread our spouses even after we have been together a long time. We judge them incorrectly and hold on to our anger. Clarify the situation and facts of a moment that sparked anger.

10. Refuse to keep thinking about the injustice.

Many couples continue to replay past problems and offenses over and over in their minds, playing particular attention to moments they were treated unfairly. This does not allow for healing and only brings back the ill-feelings you experienced at the time of the offense. Let it go. Don't get stuck in anger. Remember you will know that you have fully forgiven an offense when you stop replaying the hurtful memories in your mind. Angry, cynical people die young. Men who score high for hostility on standard tests are four times more likely to die prematurely than men whose scores are low. Doctors from Coral Gables, Florida, compared the efficiency of the heart's pumping action in 27 men.

Each of the study participants underwent one physical stress test (riding an exercise bicycle) and three mental stress tests (doing math problems in their heads, recalling a recent incident that had made them very angry, and giving a short speech to defend themselves against a hypothetical charge of shoplifting). Using sophisticated X-ray techniques, the doctors took pictures of the subjects' hearts in action during these tests. For all the subjects, anger reduced the amount of blood that the heart pumped to body tissues more than the other tests.

> All athletes are disciplined in their training. They do it to win a prize that will fade away, but we do it for an eternal prize. So I run with purpose in every step. I am not just shadowboxing. I discipline my body like an athlete, training it to do what it should. Otherwise, I fear that after preaching to others I myself might be disqualified.
>
> - 1 Corinthians 9:25-27, NLT

If we are to be what God called us all to be, if we are to live a life that is pleasing to God, if we are to live in peace and prosperity of soul and spirit, we must learn to *tame* our temper.

Repairing Your Relationship
8 Step Process

We live in a very busy world that can pull on you in so many different directions. Add to this the everyday challenges that come along with living together with another person with different backgrounds and habits, and you can find yourself struggling to maintain your joy. Marriage can be the most satisfying thing in the world if given its due attention. If you have experienced setbacks that have left open wounds and you still feel like you are walking wounded, here are some good tips.

1. Stabilization

Before you can actively repair your relationship, you must remove any negative influences that are harming the relationship. These include drinking, drugs, flirting, harmful relationships outside your marriage, inappropriate texting, inappropriate use of social media, bad friendships, and anything that is becoming a hindrance. You must work toward increasing security, safety and serenity in your marriage.

2. Reconnection

Get to know each other again. Don't just talk about your relationship, devote time to the relationship. Have casual and fun 'happy hour" chats, do friendship building activities, start a project together, take walks, and communicate with each other openly and frequently. This will start you on the road to reconnecting.

3. Act with Fondness and Admiration

Express appreciation, increase gratitude and positive communication. Praise your partner for doing well, show affection, respect and love for everyday life. Make your spouse feel safe and liked. You will be surprised how much of a difference it makes in the life of your partner when they feel appreciated and admired.

4. Deepen Your Emotional Connection

Make conscious deposits into your partners' emotional bank account, ask what you need to do to make him/her feel better, work as a team, trust your partner, and open up about your sore spots. Allow your partner to tap into your heart and mind.

5. Create a Friendly & Reassuring Environment

Manage and reduce stress, challenge your stressful / anxious/nervous thoughts. Do whatever is necessary to make your home a place of refuge, safety, comfort, and laughter. Don't let the cares of the world choke out the joy and fun God intended your home to have.

6. Manage Conflict and Hurt Feelings

Make it a practice to communicate calmly about your problems and concerns. Practice fair fighting, soften your approach, learn what it takes to sooth each other and take responsibility for your actions that will be appreciated by your partner. Do more things on the "Do" list, watch out for behaviors from the "Don't" list and try to minimize them.

7. Create a Shared Mission and Future

Establish an open line of communication and create mutual goals in life and ministry. Make plans, discuss shared future dreams, act in ways that honor each other. Got kids? Make sure to create an atmosphere and training platform for their future lives.

8. Avoid Relapse

As busy as life and ministry can be, spend time together (2.5 hours a week minimum), express gratitude and appreciation often, follow the magic 5/1 rule: For every one negative comment, make sure to make five positive comments. Talk about things that matter without having to raise your voice. Check in with each other often to make sure you are on the right track and everything is okay.

Please take time to pray this prayer:

Lord Jesus, help me to maintain solid rules of engagement whenever there is conflict in my marriage. I am determined to control my spirit and my actions, and take full responsibility for them. Help me to look to you as the only one who can fully meet all my needs. I pray that there would be found in me a desire to resolve any conflict between me and my spouse and be part of the solution rather than part of the problem. Let me never resort to profanity no matter how intense the situation may seem. I pray all of this in the name of my Lord and Savior Jesus Christ. Amen.

Chapter 5
Forgive and Forget

PEOPLE CAN HURT you. It's one of those basic facts of life. Unfortunately, one of the people who can hurt you the most is your spouse. Why? They are with you the most. They know you the best. And they know how to push your buttons (they have your pin number and have an easy access to what's locked up inside you). Whether your significant other means to or not, they will hurt you in big ways and small ways, probably many times. It could just be an offhanded comment not meant to hurt you; or it could be a major betrayal such as cheating. The point is, it happens probably more often than we would like. And the flipside is also true; we can cause hurt to our significant other as well. If you are in a relationship, hurt is inevitable. You must learn to forgive. It's part of the deal. And while you may not have an easy time forgiving now, with some practice, you can get better at it.

Yes, forgiving can in some ways be like riding a bike. There is a steep learning curve, but once you figure it out, and do it often, it does get easier. Of course, you still can get hurt along the way, but you can still keep getting back on the bike again. A healthy marriage depends upon the ability and willingness to forgive and forget offenses. One translation for the word "forgiveness" in the Bible is "to send forth." When you eat, does the body retain 100% of the food you eat? No. The human body retains the nutrients and discards the waste material. There is an awful lot of stuff we take in when we involve ourselves in a long-term relationship: some good, some not so good. If you retain all of the stuff you see, hear, and communicate without an outlet, you can get spiritually sick. One preacher referred to unforgiveness as "spiritual

78

constipation." If we keep inside us the stuff that God wants us to get rid of, it will inevitably make us sick. I see people who have come for counseling wearing a sour look on their faces as they struggle to forgive. An unwillingness to forgive manifests in many different ways including physical ailments. Consider this chapter of the book a "spiritual laxative." Think about it for a moment. When you are living with a spirit of offense and fail to forgive someone, who is really being affected the most? You are. That person is out there somewhere eating a hamburger while you battle with indigestion, can't sleep soundly, bitter, upset, critical, nervous, sick even All this happens as a result of unforgiveness. Forgiveness is like inhaling and exhaling. When you breathe in, your body is taking in Oxygen (O_2). When you exhale, carbon dioxide (CO_2) is released. As such, when you choose to forgive, you are choosing to release the toxins from your spirit, including the hurtful memories. How do you know if you have forgiven someone? We covered this briefly in the last chapter, but when you stop revisiting the memory of offense over and over in the recess of your mind, then you have forgiven. The old saying "forgive and forget" has quite a bit of truth to it. As offenses come up, I must remind myself of these principles.

Whenever I think about a person who has offended me and began to replay the resentful memories, I have succumbed to the enemy of my soul and come under the bondage of it. I choose to forgive. I forgive relatives, friends, church people, pastors, neighbors, work associates, etc. who have hurt me. I choose to do this so that I can maintain an open line of communication with my Savior and keep the plumbing clear for a generous flow of God's Spirit through me. Call upon the cleansing streams of the Holy Spirit when you fall short of personal strength to overcome offenses. Unforgiveness clogs up the plumbing between you and your God.

Be Free to Forgive

Desire: I want to be free to forgive.
Obstacle: I withhold forgiveness because I've been hurt or am angry.
Solution: I choose to forgive.
Outcome: I am now free to experience the fullness of marriage with my soul mate.

Marriage Fire Code

Marriage has been called the *union of two good forgivers.* When you constantly rub shoulders, it is impossible not to rub one another the wrong way once in a while. As marriage partners, we miscommunicate, misunderstand, and miss the sexual cues given by our partner. So what does God want us to do when our spouse has been selfish, insensitive, and demanding? Forgive!

Levels of Forgiveness

Level 1: Detached forgiveness—There is a reduction in negative feelings toward the offender, but no reconciliation takes place.

Level 2: Limited forgiveness—There is a reduction in negative feelings toward the offender, and the relationship is partially restored.

Level 3: Full forgiveness—There is a total end of negative feelings toward the offender, and the relationship is fully restored.

Forgiveness is not an approval of what they did; excusing what they did; justifying what they did; denying what they did; or blindness to what they did or pretending we're not hurt.

Forgiveness is being aware of what they did and still forgiving them; choosing to keep no records of wrongs; refusing to punish; not telling what they did; being merciful, graciousness; and the absence of bitterness. What happens when a husband or wife faces the ultimate rejection—the decision of their mate to have an affair? How do we forgive when the pain thrusts like a knife and cuts to the core of our masculinity and femininity? It may seem impossible, but it's not.

"Lord, how often shall my brother (spouse) sin against me and I forgive (him/her)? Up to seven times? Jesus said to him, "I do not say to you, up to seven times, but up to seventy times seven"
- Matthew 18:21 (Parenthesis Mine)

490 times? That's a lot of times to forgive offenses, especially if it's by the same person. Being run over by someone in a car is one thing, but when they put the car in reverse to make sure the job is done, that's hard to deal with.

Yet, God gives us the strength to forgive and forget multiple offenses. When your strength is unequal to the task, tap into *God's strength*. Remember, God does not frustrate Himself by asking us to do something we cannot do. As He calls us to forgive, He had made that capability available to us all. God asks us to forgive our spouse because He understands that without forgiveness, the flame of love dies; bitterness and resentment extinguish it. It strikes me funny that Peter suggests the number seven when asking Jesus how many times he should forgive those who trespass against us. Why seven? Well, probably because that's an easy number to count to.

I believe Peter was actually saying to Jesus, "Once I have been burned/offended seven times, number eight gives me the green light to go off on that person. When Peter suggests the number seven as the limit of offenses, Jesus tells him, "No, it will be more like seven times seventy (490 times).

Why? Because nobody in their right mind will keep track of offenses that extensively. The normal person will lose count somewhere along the way.

> See to it that no one comes short of the grace of God; that no root of bitterness springing up causes trouble, and by it many be defiled.
>
> - Hebrews 12:15

Often husbands and wives say, "I have tried to forgive. I think I've forgiven, but then when the images come again, I wonder if I really have." Every couple knows the agony of making the choice to forgive. It would help if your spouse would fall on the floor at your feet with tears, begging for forgiveness and then, as a sign of deep repentance, run out and buy you a new car in your favorite color whenever he or she offends you.

But God says we are to forgive men even if the person has not asked for forgiveness. He says, "Forgive *as* you have been forgiven." Forgive unconditionally, forgive freely and forgive repeatedly. Apologizing clears the air and offers a new beginning. When there is a problem and your spouse is the one to blame, don't demand your rights. The Bible says: *"we have been crucified with Christ,"* and dead men have no rights. Be humble in Jesus name. Offer the cup of forgiveness to the one who has offended you. When you say, "I'm sorry," relationships are mended.

Remember: love always dictates offering forgiveness when wounded. Selfish lovers hold a grudge and use it as a weapon against their mate. It's not easy to forgive, it fights the flesh. To forgive requires humility, grace, self-sacrifice and sometimes mercy.

Watch and pray, that ye enter not into temptation: the spirit indeed is willing, but the flesh is weak.

- Matthew 26:41

Blessed are the pure in heart: for they shall see God.

- Matthew 5:8

According to this Beatitude there are things that can stop you from seeing God. In other words, you may never see a mighty move of God in your life until you let offenses go. Your next personal revival may be one prayer of forgiveness away. We must not fall because someone or something has attacked us! How can we be the recipients of God's blessing when we carry unforgiveness in our hearts? Stop worrying so much about what other people say about you. If I've said it once, I'd say it again a hundred times: "It's not what people say about you that matters; it's who God says you are, and how you view yourself that makes all the difference!

Jesus asked the disciples who do *you* say that I am? They responded, "Well, some say you're this, and some say you're a prophet, teacher…" Jesus said, *"But who do you say that I am?"* Peter responded: *"I know who you are, you're the Christ, the son of the living God."* Jesus then commends Peter for his response and says, *"flesh and blood has not revealed this to you but my Father which is in heaven."* He was telling Peter, "You've got it." *"And upon this rock will I build my church and the gates of heaven shall not prevail against it."* If you can say, "You're the Messiah, my healer, my Savior, my reason for living", then you're going to survive any attack by anybody, anytime. To illustrate true forgiveness, I have chosen one of the best examples in the Bible: Joseph. A man who, in my opinion, developed a master's degree in forgiveness. Joseph was tested in the area of forgiveness and came out of the other end victorious and gracious. Joseph had a dream (from God) that he was going to be someone great.

His brothers were jealous and threw him in the pit to be sold as a slave. Have you ever been thrown under the bus by someone you thought loved you after having shared your dream with them? Yet, despite everything that took place at the time, Joseph was able to say,

> "But as for you, you thought evil against me; but God meant it for good..."
>
> - Genesis 50:20

What an attitude. What a healthy perspective, what faith and insight he must have had to say that no matter what people said or did to him, he knew God had a greater plan! Let's take a closer look at this story:

1) After being sold into slavery by his own brothers, Joseph finds himself serving at Potiphar's house as a servant.

2) After her own advances, Potiphar's wife lies about Joseph to her husband, and falsely accuses him of attempted rape.

3) Because of that lie, Joseph is sent to prison.

4) While in prison, Joseph helps people, only to have them forget all about his good works as soon as they get out.

5) Through Joseph's struggles, God remembered him, raised him up, delivered him, and brought him out of prison.

Fast forward: Joseph is now out of prison and prospering in Egypt as the prime minister, and gets married.

> And to Joseph were born two sons before the years of famine came, whom Asenath, the daughter of Poti-Pherah priest of On, bore to him. Joseph called the name of the firstborn Manasseh: "For God has made me forget all my toil and all my father's house"
>
> - Genesis 41:50

Unlike now, names were very important in the Old Testament. Names were usually given prophetically or hopefully. In the Bible days, your name made a statement, forged your future, and made a proclamation: *"And Joseph called the name of the firstborn Manasseh..." (v51).* Why? Because the name Manasseh in Hebrew means "causing to forget." *"For God has made me forget all my toil and all my father's house* (i.e. family that came against me)." This was Joseph's way of concluding in his heart of heart, 'I'm naming my first baby Manasseh because I want the devil to know that I have forgiven. I'm not going to hold offenses against me anymore. I've sent it forth. I've released it.'

Let's read on: *And the name of the second he called Ephraim for God has caused me to be fruitful in the land of my affliction" (v52).* Joseph was basically *saying,* 'I'm going to name my second born Ephraim, because even though I underwent some horrible situations because of members of my own family, I still have faith that God will bless me and see me through. The name Ephraim in Hebrew means that I shall receive double portions of blessing. In other words, Joseph was saying, "Every time you call out or read about my sons, it will be a testimony to how God has helped me "forget my toil/affliction" and now "I shall receive double portions of blessing." Joseph refused to let what people have done to him affect him to the point of giving up on them or God. His son Manasseh became a constant reminder that God has birthed in him the capacity to forgive and forget his travail (ordeal), and his other son Ephraim a reminder that he shall receive double portions of blessing for being able to move on.

Your marriage will constantly put your willingness and ability to forgive to the test. In times when you are offended or hurt by your spouse, God wants you to birth a *Manasseh* (I have forgiven) and then experience an *Ephraim* (now I shall be doubly blessed). Joseph forgave his brothers, loved them, blessed them, and was able to celebrate every family reunion from that point on. To forgive and forget offenses in your marriage is an acquired ability, but well worth the effort. Publilius Syrus once said, "It is foolish to punish your neighbor by fire when you live next door." To live together in peace and harmony is something we all seek and is attainable no matter what challenges we face. How are we to forgive others? Let's dissect something commonly referred to as "Our Father." *After this manner* therefore pray ye:

> Our Father which art in heaven, Hallowed be thy name. Thy kingdom come. Thy will be done in earth, as it is in heaven. Give us this day our daily bread. And forgive us our debts, as we forgive our debtors...
> - Matthew 6:9-12

As for *v12*, some translations say, *"...forgive our trespasses as we forgive those who trespass against us..."* (*Matt 6:9-12.*) *"...Forgive us our debts..."* How? *"...As we forgive our debtors."* Are you sure you want to pray this prayer? Do you really want God to forgive us "as" (or the same way) we forgive other people? Do you really want God to remember your offenses as long as you do others?

> "And forgive us our debts, as (the same way) we forgive our debtors. And lead us not into temptation, but deliver us from evil: For thine is the kingdom, and the power, and the glory, forever. Amen.
>
> - Matthew 6:12

Amen usually means it's over, let it be done. but look how it continues in *v14*: *For if ye forgive men their trespasses, your heavenly Father will also forgive you:* Isn't that a terrible "if"? This scripture suggests that my relationship with God might be hindered by how I treat/forgive other people. How can I tell whether or not I have truly forgiven someone? If there is anybody that can enter your sphere of influence and say something that alters your mood, your attitude, and cause you to think evil of them, you probably haven't forgiven them. Why would you give that much power to another person?

If they can affect you and change you, causing you to react, that's too much power for you to give anybody. Here's a story found in one of T.D. Jakes's sermons:

> There was a Christian woman who died and found herself at the pearly gates of Heaven, and the first person she saw there was St. Peter (still trying to find out why people always refer to Peter at the gate). At any rate, she was ecstatic about making it to Heaven and said, "May I enter?" Peter said "Yes, you have been found in the book of life, but there's just one thing you must do to enter in. You must spell "Heaven." "Oh, praise God, that's an easy one: H-E-A-V-E-N," she answered. But just as she began passing through, Peter said, "Oh wait just a second, the Master is calling me and I must go immediately. Will you do me a huge favor? In my absence if anybody else makes it this far, can you give them the same routine I gave you to enter in?" "Sure, I'm so

excited to have my very first heavenly assignment here," the woman answered. Just a moment later, the woman noticed a figure making its way through the clouds, "Yes, it's my first person I get to allow in!" She was excited, but as the figure came closer, there emerged a man. "Oh no, it's my ex-husband!" She was dismayed. Well, he approached the woman and said, "You made it here?" She answered with a question: "You made it here too?" Her ex-husband said, "Move over and let me in." The woman said "Stop! Wait a minute. Before you enter through these gates, you have to do one thing." "What's that?" He asked. The woman with a sneer on her face told him, "You must spell 'Czechoslovakia.'"

We must *all* learn to forgive and forget.

10 Forgiveness Tips

1) Make the decision to forgive.

2) Realize that it is good for you to let go.

Acknowledge that forgiveness is not about letting someone off the hook, but about freeing yourself so that you can fully get on with your life. This gives you the motivation to move forward. Acknowledge that forgiveness will benefit your mental and emotional health, as well as the health of your heart, helping you face the days ahead with joy. Medical science has linked many illnesses (mental and physical) to harboring offenses in your heart and mind. Forgiveness is actually good for you.

3) Develop empathy.

Empathy (in simple terms) is feeling someone else's pain. Acknowledge that you too, may have hurt people in the past, and from this train of thought try to develop some empathy for the person who has hurt you (if that is possible—if the transgression was not too severe). Could their behavior have been the result of some way they have been hurt in the past? Could they have had a bad childhood, for instance? Could they have now changed, as you might have done? When we develop empathy, it makes forgiveness much easier.

4) Write a letter to the person who has hurt you (but *don't* post it).

This is about getting things off your chest. Write about how you feel, how you were hurt, and say what you would like to say to the person. Imagine talking to them face-to-face and finish by saying that you are choosing to let go now and move on with your life, and that you wish them well with theirs. It's important to get stuff off your chest but to finish on a positive note. You can turn this into a ritual and have a "letting go" party, where you and some friends might burn your letters.

5) Take a positive action.

This is about doing something positive that demonstrates to yourself that you have moved on. What have you not done because you have been holding onto the past? Could you do it now? I have recently decided to contact people who have been upset with me or the ministry, and simply reach across the table and shake their hands. Not to discuss the offense but just to say "Hey, I still value you in spite of any differences we might have had in the past." The result has been phenomenal.

6) Take a moment.

When we are hurt, many times we are too emotional in that moment to react in an appropriate manner. So when your spouse or partner hurts you, step back and take a breath. Even remove yourself from their presence if you need to. You can certainly say, "That really hurt me," but refrain from letting your emotions get the best of you. It's better to take a moment to collect your thoughts before really discussing the matter. Take a whole day if you need to. Just let it mull over in the back of your mind. Sleep on it. A new day may bring a new perspective. Time may provide the calmness you need.

7) Focus on what's important.

Weigh in on this *every time* your spouse intentionally/ unintentionally inflicts an emotional wound: is justice more important, or is the relationship more important? Sometimes when we are hurt, justice is all we can think about. We feel we are right, our spouse is wrong, and we must have the wrong be made right. Why do we think this way? Emotional wounds have a way of making us turn inward and assessing the situation only from our side of things. We think that somehow justice will make us feel better. But does it actually make us feel better? Not really. The question is then, what actually helps heal the hurt? The answer is forgiving, forgetting, and moving past the situation. If we don't forgive, then we can't move forward. We get stuck. No relationship can survive if you can't progress.

8) Discuss the issue at hand.

When you are both ready, you need to sit down and talk about what had happened. Be calm and *take turns*. Really listen to what they are saying instead of just taking that time to formulate a backlash. You may think you have all of the information, but you may not. Look at this as a time of learning. Go into it with an attitude of love. Also, be careful not to bring other issues into the discussion. Stay focused, speak your peace, and be calm and loving.

9) *Actually* forgive and forget.

Just as important as it is to hear the words, "I'm sorry," your significant other also needs to hear the words, "I forgive you" from you. Be sincere. When you forgive, it means you actually are letting the other person know that you are not holding a grudge or harboring the issue for later use. While forgiving is one thing, forgetting is another. You certainly won't "forget" but you can get past it. How? By letting go of the hurt that doesn't define either of you or your relationship. Look forward, not backwards. Only then can your relationship truly heal.

10) Ask for help.

Be real and come to God knowing that you are not Him. There is only so much we can accomplish with the arm of the flesh. We need God to go beyond our own ability to forgive. Ask God who freely gives that which we ask for. Ask friends, true friends for help and added prayer. True friends and loved ones will tell you the truth about yourself. You will be amazed by how much can be accomplished through prayer. One of the greatest things about prayer is that it helps us do some soul searching and realize that forgiveness really is a choice.

Bottom line: Unforgiveness has been the cause of countless divorces, violence, revenge, anger, pain, physical and emotional illness. Let's make a decision to forgive all who have offended us, particularly our spouse.

Please take time to pray this prayer:

Lord Jesus, help me to forgive my spouse whenever I feel offended, keeping in mind how much you have forgiven me. Help me to never harbor resentment or seek revenge, but instead seek healing and restoration. I pray for the ability to forgive and forget, and renounce any root of bitterness. Lord, give me empathy for my spouse whenever I feel angry or offended. I pray all of this in the name of my Lord and Savior Jesus Christ. Amen.

Chapter 6
Things That Go Bump in the Night

"THINGS THAT GO bump in the night" is the last line from Scottish Prayer: "From ghoulies and ghosties and long-legged beasties / and things that go bump in the night, / good Lord, deliver us!" It was also a Broadway play in 1965. The play depicts a vaguely apocalyptic and futuristic family transformed by fear, living in their basement, and treating each other with suspicion, threats, and contempt. But for the sake of this book and its subject matter, "things that go bump in the night" are the memories that still hurt, those things that still cause pain and discomfort in your life even years after it happened. Memories of abandonment, abuse, ridicule, severe criticism, hatred, or prejudice that just tore you down. Quite often these experiences haunt you well into adulthood and manifest in dreams, cause insecurity, depression and fear. One of the latest surveys revealed that one out of every four people in America has experienced sexual abuse.

There is also physical abuse, emotional abuse, and the pain associated with the loss of a loved one. The fact is, most of us have had setbacks like these. You may be masking it, but we all have them. Over time, I have learned that emotional scars take longer to heal than physical wounds. God has lots of names to describe who He is and what He does, one of them is "Jehovah Rapha," which means "I am the God who heals". The Bible says,

> "God heals the brokenhearted and bandages their wounds."

> - Psalm 147:3, NCV

You say, "How does He do that? Is there a process? How do I sign up for this type of healing?

"...God anointed Jesus of Nazareth with the Holy Spirit and with power, who went about doing good and healing all who were oppressed by the devil, for God was with Him"

- Acts 10:38

So, the first step begins when I *come* to Jesus with my pain, sorrow, and issues. You're never going to get well until you face your feelings head on. You would be surprised how many people I counsel who stuff all of life's problems deep inside their hearts to a point where they are like emotional pressure cookers. If there is no relief valve or outlet to blow off some steam, there will be a blow out. Look what David in the Bible said about this:

"I kept very quiet but I became even more upset. I became very angry inside, and as I thought about it, my anger burned"

- Psalm 39:2-3, NCV

He's saying when you keep everything inside, it only grows and burns hotter. They fester and don't go away. It just makes it worse. Did you know that one of the causes of constant fatigue is because you're using up emotional energy on resentments, grudges, guilts and griefs of your past?

"When I kept things to myself, I felt weak deep inside me and I moaned all day long."

- Psalm 32:3, NCV

He's saying it's emotionally draining to keep everything inside and not confess or share your feelings with someone. We are many times haunted by past discouragements and let-downs in life, particularly when we don't vent. People respond to abuse in different ways. Some hide their feelings and pretend they don't exist, others run from it by getting drunk, taking drugs, sleeping with people that really don't care about them, become a workaholic, or blame others for their misfortune. But none of these things bring you out of the anxiety it produces.

91

Step 1 is to be honest about your pain, fear, anger, resentment and bitterness over what people did to you. Healing from things that go "bump" in the night is sharing your thoughts and feelings with someone who cares. I am not a psychologist, but did attend a training class which certified me to be part of a peer support team for critical incident stress management and post disaster recovery. The instructor, who is a psychologist, taught us that the word "therapy" in its origin came from the phrase "talk healing." She explained that when first responders encounter a traumatic incident, it can later trigger bad memories and manifest in many different harmful symptoms.

However, when you begin to talk about it to someone, there comes a release of some of the residual feelings that had been pent up inside the mind. She even said that prayer is a form of release. Immediately I referenced two things: First, I thought of the patient lying down on a recliner talking to a psychiatrist about all of their life's difficulties. After an hour of talking about everything that bothered him/her, they jump off the couch, hugged the doctor and says: "Wow, I already feel so much better, you're the best doctor I've ever met, you did good doc." In reality though, the doctor said very little. I mean no evaluation, explanation or anything else. Just lending an ear and allowing "talk healing" to take place. The second thing that popped into my mind after hearing the psychologist speak was that medical science is only now discovering these things what the Bible has been saying for hundreds and hundreds of years: *"...confess your sins to one another and be healed."*

Talk to someone about your problems and concerns. Talk to your spouse, a close friend, and of course God. Be honest with yourself, the person involved, and God. I distinctly remember that in that class that I took there were captains, paramedics and firefighters who after sharing the traumatic incidents they responded to during their career as first responders, began to weep. This is not the most macho thing to do in the presence of all your buddies and co-workers but the tears could not be held back.

"Casting all your care upon him; for he cares for you"
- 1 Peter 5:7

Why do we have to reveal our hurts/anger?

"You are only hurting yourself with your anger"
- Job 18:4, GNT

These bottled-up emotions of hurts and abuses (i.e. "bumps in the night") must be shared in order to experience freedom and peace of mind. There must be some sort of relief valve installed in your life in order to deal with the past. Next, you need to forgive those who have offended you. Let go of the resentment you carry deep inside. Releasing is always better than resentment. You say, "But they don't deserve to be forgiven!" Let me ask a question: Did *you* deserve to be forgiven, or has God forgiven you in spite of you? You can't get on with your life so long as you're stuck in the past. The longer you hold onto resentment, the longer that person has a control over your life. Getting revenge or having thoughts of such only haunt you further.

"Never pay back evil for evil. Never avenge yourself. Leave that to God. For He has said that He will repay those that deserve it"
- Romans 12:17,19, LB

Let's look to the ultimate example for our lives.

"When Jesus suffered, He did not threaten to get even. He left His case in the hands of God"
- 1 Peter 2:23, LB

Although there are scores of reasons for anxiety, stress, and bitterness, the things that haunt us at night can be worked out through prayer and a few action steps. This is important not only for our own peace of mind but also for your friends and family.

"A bitter spirit is not only bad in itself but can also poison the lives of many others"
- Hebrews 12:15, PB

According to this scripture, if you don't deal with the bitterness which many times attaches itself to those who don't deal with past disappointments and the demons that haunt you, it can have an adverse effect on the people around you. It is important to realize that it is not God's will for you to be tormented by a demon from the past. Nor is it His will that you lose sleep over offenses, discouragements, and setbacks from your *past*. Unfortunately, we tend to carry things like molestation, verbal abuse, abandonment, preferential treatment, mental/emotional abuse into our present relationships. This causes a huge strain on what should be a good, healthy marriage. These issues don't seem to go away with time, but are sometimes magnified. This is not the will of God for your life or that of your spouse.

> For I know the thoughts that I think toward you, says the Lord, thoughts of peace and not of evil, to give you a future and a hope
>
> - Jeremiah 29:11

We must learn to get our attention off our past and look to God's plan for our future.

> "Put your heart right, reach out to God and face the world again, firm and courageous.   Then all your troubles will fade from your memory like floods that are past and remembered no more"
>
> - Job 11:13-16, GNT

Please take time to pray this prayer:

God Almighty, I seek your power and anointing to overcome my past traumas and setbacks. I cast all my care upon you because I know that you care for me. I refuse to allow my past to dictate my future. Remind me to seek therapy through prayer and open communication with my spouse. I receive your healing and deliverance over my life and yield to your power in regards to my past. I pray for restful sleep as I gain strength through you word and promises. I pray all of this in the name of my Lord and Savior Jesus Christ. Amen.

Chapter 7
Avoiding the "D" Word

MORE THAN ANY time in history, the social disaster called divorce has climbed at an alarming rate. The fact is, the divorce rate has jumped from 10% in1960 to over 50% today. Why is it that fewer and fewer people are willing to commit themselves to their spouse for life? I often ask troubled couples this question in counseling: "What do you think is missing in our relationship? What do you think would make things better?" I have them answer this question: My marriage would be so much better if only... The same answer I hear over and over is this: "For us to have things the way they were in the beginning of our relationship, to be in love again." Isn't that what all of us really want deep down inside? To love one another and have fun together and build together.

Did you know that the United States has gone from the most marrying country in the world to the country with the most divorces and the highest number of unwed mothers in the world? I know there are lots of contributing factors for the increase in divorce today. Some of the reasons include 1) a change in our culture; 2) the availability of pornography; 3) a lack of commitment to marriage. God says,

"I hate divorce, Make sure you do not break your promise to be faithful to your mate"
- Malachi 2:16

This same verse in the Message translation Bible describes divorce as *"a violent dismembering of the 'one flesh' of marriage."* Wow, think about it. If we experience the supernatural oneness of marriage and separate that, it's like splitting the atom.

You will never be able to build a great marriage unless you throw out the option of divorce from your mind and conversation. As long as divorce is an *option*, you will tend to shun the responsibility of making things work out.

Rather than choosing to iron out the wrinkles, you'll want to revert to the "D" word. It is always easy to walk out than it is to stay and rebuild a relationship. It's always much easier to run than it is to rebuild. It is always more rewarding however, to rebuild than it is to run. Are there exceptions to all of this? Absolutely. We will cover those exceptions later in this chapter. Since the day we got married, my wife Liz and I decided that divorce is not an option for us. We locked the escape hatch on our marriage when we got married, and threw away the key. We told ourselves, 'I don't care how tough it may get from time to time, we're going to make this marriage work.' This commitment has stood the test of time of over 40 years now. When you got married, you made a promise to God, "Till death do us part." One of the reasons people don't keep commitments is because they don't know the meaning of commitment.

Commitment means being dedicated. It means that no matter how hard things get, you dedicate yourself to work it out. Your marriage is what you make it to be. We have all heard the saying, "The grass is greener on the other side." If it is, it's because it's being watered. Marriage is something that takes effort to make it great. It takes time, patience, empathy, mutual respect, love compromise, endurance, unity, vision... Not all of these things come natural to us. Too many couples would rather throw in the towel than give marriage this kind of effort. Let's look at a biblical approach to divorce and remarriage.

> The Pharisees also came to Him, testing Him, and saying to Him, "Is it lawful for a man to divorce his wife for just any reason?" And He answered and said to them, "Have you not read that He who made them at the beginning 'made them male and female,' and said, 'For this reason a man shall leave his father and mother and be joined to his wife, and the two shall become one flesh'? So then, they are no longer two but one flesh. Therefore what God has joined together, let not man separate."

They said to Him, "Why then did Moses command to give a certificate of divorce, and to put her away?"

— Matthew 19:3-7

They were referring to Deuteronomy 24:1,2, the ordinances of the law by Moses, which establishes and declares a means of divorce. The Pharisees were essentially saying, "Why then does the Bible say you can do it?" See how Jesus responds to this question:

He said to them, "Moses, because of the hardness of your hearts, permitted you to divorce your wives, but from the beginning it was not so. And I say to you, whoever divorces his wife, except for sexual immorality, and marries another, commits adultery; and whoever marries her who is divorced commits adultery." His disciples said to Him, "If such is the case of the man with his wife, it is better not to marry." But He said to them, "All cannot accept this saying, but only those to whom it has been given: For there are eunuchs who were born thus from their mother's womb, and there are eunuchs who were made eunuchs by men, and there are eunuchs who have made themselves eunuchs for the kingdom of heaven's sake. He who is able to accept it, let him accept it"

— Matthew 19:8-12

The eunuch referred to in the Bible is one that has no desire to marry. Jesus said there are some who are born without the desire. Others were made eunuchs by the hands of men—castrated. This was common practice in the courts of kings to those who were to have no distractions and would focus on service rather than a sexual relationship with a woman. There were others who have made themselves eunuchs for the kingdom of God. These felt it was important to stay single for the sake of the ministry that God had called them to. The apostle Paul makes reference to the very same thing in 1 Corinthians 7:32-33: "But I would have you without carefulness. He that is unmarried cares for the things that belong to the Lord, how he may please the Lord: But he that is married cares for the things that are of the world, how he may please his wife."

He's saying those who remain single by virtue of their commitment to ministry in their singleness have a greater availability and mobility than those who are involved in family life. One of the greatest challenges of someone married and in ministry is to give adequate time for both. Equilibrium is needed when you are married. Nowhere in the Bible is there a statement that celibacy is a requirement for effective ministry, but that there would be those who will follow a single way of life solely for greater fruitfulness in ministry. Jesus and Paul both call it a gift. If you fear it or don't think you can handle living a single life (without sex) you obviously don't have the gift! If you are divorced and are curious as to the will of God for your life, it is linked to your submission to a local body (church). Not your own whim, your own will, or even revelation. It requires submission and trust to a body.

Why does a divorced person need to submit to a church body in their decision of remarriage? Because there is no future for that person in another marriage until they first learn how to stay married in another sense—Married to the body of Christ in trust, dependence, patience and love. This is not a harsh legalistic attempt at control, but a healthy accountability.

A loving, patient discipline of the leadership of the church. It's during this time a person learns trust, which is one of the key issues that probably caused the person to leave his or her marriage in the first place. It is sometimes difficult, because it is difficult to begin a new relationship once you have had a trust breached and a commitment violated in your previous marriage. So what's God's attitude towards divorce? God doesn't like it. That doesn't blackball those that are divorced or write them off from a fulfilled life in Christ. The Pharisees approach to Jesus brings us the following:

> The Pharisees also came unto him, tempting him, and saying unto him, Is it lawful for a man to put away his wife for every cause?
>
> - Matthew 19:3

This was not an innocent inquiry, but one to trap Jesus into his own words. Similar to the same way a person would try and trap a teacher of the gospel today. There is absolutely no excuse for two people who live in Christ to arbitrarily divorce or go their own way and expect some kind of future with another person. That is not the Lord's way. This is hard for some people to hear because it requires a deep faith and submission to a living God who can work a miracle in your relationship. "Yeah, but we weren't saved when we got married, now we're having all kinds of problems, maybe I married the wrong person outside of the will of God." You're trying to make a case that maybe you should leave each other and start all over with another person. Not only is there no scripture in the Bible to warrant that, but a number of scriptures that tell us that that should not be done. The requirement in scripture is that you abide where you are. Don't follow the drum beat of the world. We don't have to feel tingly or excited about one another all the time in order to have a successful marriage. It should not be based on sexual compatibility alone, or seeing eye-to-eye all the time.

Christians have been known to say "Well, we just can't believe it's God's will for us to live this way." You're right about that, it's not God's desire to see you live in turmoil, but it's also not His will for you to be divorced unless there is infidelity. Even in that case, He wants you to learn to work things out in Him! To forgive and move forward. *"Where the spirit of the Lord is there is liberty."* Perhaps you need a stronger influence of God in your marriage. God gives no provision for you to change partners every time someone blows a whistle, every time you don't see eye-to-eye, or when you realize that he or she isn't as physically attractive as they used to be. Divorce, or the "D" word, should not be in the vocabulary of two believers in Christ. The will of God is that we learn to grow together by staying committed to the marriage, and completely dependent upon the power of the Holy Spirit.

The Proper and Improper Application of Divorce

Jesus said, *"What God put together let no man put asunder* (away)." The Pharisees said, "then why did Moses allow for divorce?" Jesus said, "It was not so from the beginning" Again we find Jesus addressing a situation without violating the law; he will not erase one portion of the law of God. –In the same manner, the scripture says:

> "it is easier for heaven and earth than the law to become null and void"
>
> - Luke 16:17

Jesus enhanced or extended the application of the law to even higher proportions. To the Pharisees' question about Moses command, "Didn't Moses say *you can divorce?*' Jesus answers, *"Yes, but he did so because of 'the hardening of your hearts' but from the beginning it was not so."* In other words, divorce is not the way He wanted it to be. The point is, God did make provision for divorce, but it wasn't His first choice for our lives. God wants us to learn to live and grow together in a marriage. To watch the power of God work out and override hardness of heart, discord, and bitterness that are in marriages, and bring true deliverance. In counseling couples on the verge of a divorce, I recommend time to allow God to work in their marriage. It requires faith on the part of the couple, but it is God's way! You too, like Pharisees, can insist, "But doesn't the law say it was possible for divorce?"

From the Bible, we see that Jesus had answered then, and will answer now with: "That's right, but it was because of hardness of heart." We believe the Lord can make hearts soft… that's why it is worth the long haul. It is at the core of our belief that He can save and heal marriages. Jesus wasn't saying, 'Who cares about your emotions? Just follow the rule or abide by the law.' He knows the possibilities of a couple or a person submitted to God. There is *nothing impossible* for God. I've seen God bring a deeper understanding to a troubled couple and bring a new meaning to a second honeymoon. Revived marriage by the power of the Holy Spirit is available to all who call upon His name (Jesus). You may say, "you don't know how difficult it is to deal with the hurt." I believe Jesus would say, "Do all you can to keep it together and allow God to bring life back to it." He said "I am the resurrection and the life."

One of the main reasons of divorce is a lack of forgiveness! People will not forgive one another. Remember: The word of God gives counsel, but the Holy Spirit gives you the power to see it through. So, in short, if you want to live according to the letter of the law and not the spirit, you can get a divorce. Jesus said however,

> "But I tell you that anyone who divorces his wife, except for marital unfaithfulness, causes her to become an adulteress, and anyone who marries the divorced woman commits adultery"
>
> - Matthew 5:32

If there has been a breach of trust to the point of immorality, and the violated in the relationship feels they can never trust again, God gives them a backdoor called divorce. Yet, He gives us counsel to stay together if at all possible and provides scriptural examples of sticking it out in the Bible. God told a prophet named Hosea, 'I want to teach you something about my heart towards a whoring nation (Israel), a nation that cheats on me.' *"Like an unfaithful woman they have given themselves over to other gods."* Their worship to those false gods was viewed by God as being unfaithful and cheating. He said they've gone after those manmade gods. God told Hosea, "I want you to marry a woman who has sold herself to many lovers."

Can you imagine that! Hosea was instructed by God to marry a harlot, a prostitute. Hosea, a man who was anointed to bring forth God's message, a holy man of God, the mouthpiece of God. Why? So the prophet would understand at firsthand how God felt every time his bride would cheat on Him. Secondly, Hosea was given a lesson on grace, mercy and forgiveness. Subsequently, Hosea preached with true passion. The lesson: The Lord teaches his grace to accept an unfaithful people. *"I will receive you again unto myself."* He teaches us to be Christian (Christ like) in our forgiveness towards one another. God can teach us such a degree of forgiveness that we would never have to exercise the privilege that the letter of the law allows in verse nine of our text: *"If your partner is guilty of sexual immorality you can if you must file for divorce" (v9).* Let's explore the exceptions.

As a counseling Pastor, I have had cases where there was violence, extreme verbal abuse, dangerous insanity, and other factors that made it impossible to live with a spouse without constant anxiety, stress, clinical depression, fear for one's life, child abuse etc. Let me be clear and concise: God does not expect anyone to endure this level of abuse for any length of time. There is the letter of the law and the spirit of the law. Again, if one gives a good effort to reconcile and forgive, and this level of abuse is experienced or continues, I say run before the situation escalates and results in further abuse. I have counseled several women in my years of pastoring that experienced hair loss, nightmares, fear, anxiety, constant crying spells and even thoughts of suicide because of the abuse suffered by their husbands. They haven't cheated, just literally drove them to the very edge of doom.

How About Remarriage?

Although this chapter is dedicated to avoiding divorce, what if we have been divorced and are looking to re-marry? Or should a divorcee hold a position of ministry in the church? We know what scripture says about it. It says that anyone in church leadership must be the husband of one wife.

A bishop then must be blameless, the husband of one wife, vigilant, sober, of good behavior, given to hospitality, apt to teach.

- 1 Timothy 3:2

Let the deacons be the husbands of one wife, ruling their children and their own houses well.

- 1 Timothy 3:12

If any be blameless, the husband of one wife, having faithful children not accused of riot or unruly.

- Titus 1:6

Well, that eliminates 90% of us, doesn't it? Not necessarily. There is a place in ministry for everyone in the body of Christ, but to be a leader of the flock God had entrusted us with, we should be a clear reflection of His commitment to us. He is faithful! We as Christians must remain faithful in marriage *for life*. Is there any leeway in that? You bet! *"if any man be in Christ he is a new creature."* In short, if you were divorced before coming to a saving knowledge of Christ, I believe there should be leadership opportunities for the same reason we have allowed for others in spite of other sins. Divorce should not be practiced as a Christian unless there has been unfaithfulness and the innocent cannot reconcile or get through the offense after an honest effort. If you have a broken marriage in your past, remember, you are now a new creature in Christ! The word of God provides the opportunity for us as Christians to experience fulfillment in life and ministry even if you've been divorced three times.

But as a Christian, we know that God desires for us to stick it out and *trust Him* for a miracle of restoration. If your heart has been broken or hardened from divorce, let God heal you. The word of God was never intended to take a person and slice out a whole segment of their lives by saying,

"O.K. you've had your one chance and blown it, now you're doomed for the rest of your life," or "If you're a Christian, you'll never be able to get married again." No! That's the letter of the law. But Pastor, how about verse nine: *"If your partner is guilty of sexual immorality you can if you must file for divorce."* Well, what about it? First of all, let's look at who Christ was addressing and under what condition.

The Pharisees who asked this question didn't want an answer, they were there to taunt and tempt Jesus. However, they did want to justify their own carnal desires. The same Pharisees who turned the sabbath into a binding law which didn't even leave room for God to be God, now attempts to do the same thing with divorce and re-marriage. They would now use the word of God to justify their desire to get rid of their wives whenever they wanted a new wife (*"Is it lawful for a man to divorce his wife for just any reason?"* (v3)). Taking the word of God, they would have liked to shove it in her face and say, "See woman, the Bible says I can." Do you think that is what God intended? Of course not. 'Another woman understands me better, so I'm going to play marital hopscotch.' 'She looks better, she works harder, she's more affectionate, she meets my needs, we get along so much easier than my husband/wife.' You backslidden Pharisee! Jesus said, "You are putting away your partner for the sake of marrying another." It is the spirit of the world! There is a stroke of insanity by the hand of the devil which will cause us to think, 'Well, maybe she is the one God really intended for me.

After all, I was young when I married, or we were drunk at the time, and didn't really know what we were doing." The idea is to get out of this marriage to get into this other one. Jesus said, "That's adultery." You're violating the word of God, so it's adultery! By doing this you, short circuit the will and power of God to reconcile the relationship. God's desire is total healing and health in a marital relationship.

In Jesus, there is revelation of hearts being made soft enough to where all marriages have hope. For this reason, it is wise for divorcees to come under the submission of the church in their healing and restoration. If there is even a remote opportunity for reconciliation in a separation of couples, it should be sought. Not by a law written somewhere, but the will of God and a maturity to attempt to reconcile. Because there are different cases, that's where the submission to the church comes into play. It's in a *healthy* church that we learn the way of forgiveness and trust again. The Lord does say that in a divorce situation that you have a responsibility to walk in obedience to the body of Jesus Christ. To have a loving, scripture based, compassionate, and honest pastor to be accountable to is a huge advantage.

My counsel to most people who are either going through a divorce or recently divorced is to not seek another relationship for six to twelve months. This makes sure that the seeds of the last failure have been rooted out, as it takes time. Don't barge into another relationship right away; give God time to heal and cleanse you. Can God put together what man has split asunder? I believe so. One of the many marriage miracles I have witnessed was a couple who attended my church many years ago. The church was experiencing revival, and God was adding to the church each week. However, in the midst of this move of God, one of the couples whom I had known for over 25 years had run into some very deep-rooted problems. What started out as delving into pornography eventually materialized into an affair. Divorce took place, and ten years (after rehabilitation and pastoral counsel) later, they were able to come back together, rededicate their lives to Christ, and remarry. They remain married to this day and are expected to grow old gracefully together.

The bottom line is that there is always hope where there is life in Christ. Having said all of this, I still want to communicate that there are still valid reasons to get divorced. This may almost sound contradictory to this whole chapter, but be reminded that if there is a situation where you have tried over and over, prayed over and over, and you still have not the capacity to trust again and live at an acceptable level of peace, God gave you a back door called divorce. Again, God is a miracle worker as long as we give Him the opportunity to speak into our situation. Let me share with you some reasons why marriages do not work. I have ministered on this subject for over 25 years and have a long list of principles, tips, suggestions and experience on the subject.

That is why I am writing this book. To place in your hands information to preserve the sanctity of your marriage and fulfill the will of God together with your spouse. It saddens me to note that according to recent statistics, over half of the people who get married in America today end up in divorce. The million-dollar question? Why? Well, this book will not be able to contain all the reasons why divorce has hit epidemic proportions but I'm trying to cover as much as possible.

Reasons Why Marriages Fail

1. Selfishness

I covered this subject much more extensively back in chapter 2 (the marriage miracle) but feel it is important to mention it again. I believe at the core of marital failure you will find a self-centered person(s). It is one of the biggest killers of marriage today. I know selfishness sounds pretty vague but at the core of most marital failure is an over emphasis on the self, what *I* want or don't want. Statements like "What's important to you will is important to me" is the furthest thing from the truth to a self-centered individual. A selfish relationship is always one sided and never allows for teamwork or growth. There is such a thing as being so full of yourself that there is no more room for anyone else. Marriage is all about give and take. Love ventilates itself through giving. If you are a taker (and I've met several takers in my time), there is nothing you will be able to do to fill your void. You are subconsciously living only for yourself and on a quest to fill a void that can never be filled. No one can love you enough, give you enough, satisfy you enough… Your selfishness creates a vacuum that your spouse will never be able to fill. Your significant other will soon grow weary of serving you and ending up with the short end of the stick. Selfishness is a killer of marriages.

2. Social Media

That's right, social media. In recent years, we have experienced a social media explosion. We're more connected than ever before, but completely disconnected at the same time. Let's face it: the last time you "spoke" to the person you love, you didn't even hear their voice. Instead of good face-to-face communication, there is text, email, voicemail, twitter, facebook, instagram, snap chat, etc. There's no physical connection attached to anything anymore. We've developed relationships with things, not each other. 95% of the personal conversations you have on a daily basis occur through some type of technology. We've removed human emotion from our relationships. Somehow, we've learned to get offended by text on a screen, accusing others of being "angry" or "sad," when in fact, we have no idea what they are feeling. We argue about this at length. We've forgotten how to communicate, yet expect healthy marriages. How is it possible to grow and mature together if we barely speak? Today, if someone doesn't text you back within 30 minutes, they're suddenly cheating on you. You want to know why your grandmother and grandfather just celebrated their 60th wedding anniversary? Because they weren't scrolling through Instagram worrying about what John ate for dinner. They weren't on Facebook criticizing others. They weren't on vacation sending Snapchats to their friends. No. They were too preoccupied loving and respecting one another. They were talking to each other at dinner, walking with each other holding hands instead of their phones. They weren't distracted by everything around them. They had dreams and chased them together.

No longer is our battle for identity falsely portrayed by Hollywood alone, now we have the capability of emotional affairs brought to us with a simple tapping of our fingers on our computers and smartphones. I know a married couple who had been married for almost 40 years, and have recently divorced over an affair that started over contact made to an old high school sweetheart on Facebook. What a wonderful thing technology can be, but it has also served as an avenue for reconnecting with past lovers and high school heartthrobs. We have been given the power to contact people that we never would have found outside of the social media tools we now have available. Social media is like fire. It can warm you or burn you. Use it wisely and take caution of its power to destroy if used inappropriately. I have been amazed by how many people (including middle age couples) have ultimately thrown away years of fruitfulness, trust, and love by yielding to the temptation of making unlawful connections with the opposite sex—relationships that had long been appropriately forgotten. Check out this excerpt from article written by Anthony D'Ambrosio. I read a while back concerning social media:

> Social media has given everyone an opportunity to be famous. Attention you couldn't dream of getting unless you were celebrity is now a selfie away. Post a picture, and thousands of strangers will like it. Wear less clothing, and guess what? More likes. It's more than that though. What about the life you live? I see

pictures of people decked out in designer clothes, eating at fancy expensive restaurants or at amusement parks taking advantage of all they have to offer—people that I know are dead broke. But they portray themselves as successful because, well, they can. And they get this gratification from people who like and comment on their statuses or pictures. If you want to love someone, stop seeking attention from everyone because you'll never be satisfied with the attention from one person. Same holds true for love. Love is supposed to be sacred. You can't love someone when you're preoccupied with worrying about what others think of you. Whether it be posting pictures on social media, buying homes to compete with others or going on lavish vacations - none of it matters. Social media just invited a few thousand people into what should be your personal life. We've thrown privacy out the window these days. Nothing is sacred anymore, in fact, it's splattered all over the Web for the world to see. Everywhere we go, everything we do - made public. Instead of enjoying the moment, we get lost in cyberspace, trying to figure out the best status update, or the perfect filter. Something as simple as enjoying breakfast with your spouse has become a photo shoot. Vacations are no longer a time to relax, but more a time to post vigorously. You can't just sit back and soak it all in. There's absolutely nothing wrong with sharing moments of your life. I do it myself. But where do we draw the line? When does it become too much? We've invited strangers into our homes and brought them on dates with us. We've shown them our wardrobe, drove with them in our cars, and we even showed them our bathing suits. Might as well pack them a suitcase, too. Marriage is sacred. It is the most beautiful sacrament God has created and has tremendous promise for those fortunate enough to experience it. I am a believer in true love and building a beautiful life with someone. I hope you never experience the demise of your love. It's painful, and life changing; something nobody should ever feel. I fear that the world we live in today has put roadblocks in the way of getting there and living a happy life with someone.

Marriage Fire Code

A lot of things to consider.

3. Too Much or Too Little Emphasis on the Physical Aspect of the Relationship

If you come into marriage for sex alone, you will be disappointed. You may argue that statement by saying, "Speak for yourself," but in reality, sex is very brief when compared to the amount of time spent together doing other things. Although doing life together should include sex, it's not the ingredient that keeps you together through trying times or meets the deep-rooted needs of your partner. Besides, the more time that goes by in years, "intimacy" develops into "into me you see." Most men don't really know what intimacy is until they reach about 40-years-old. Before then, it's sex and sex alone. As time goes by and your relationship matures, you should experience a deeper appreciation and love toward each other beyond the "take care of my needs" stage that sex only brings. The relationship aspect becomes deeper and deeper, and you become less dependent on feelings. On the other hand, if sex becomes almost non-existent it can create a myriad of other problems.

Beyond being pleasurable, sex connects two individuals. According the Bible, it is the element that actually consummates a marriage. There's a reason why it's referred to as making love or two becoming one. There's just something about touching someone, kissing someone, feeling someone that should make your hair stand up. I'm baffled by couples who neglect having sex, especially younger couples. I remember when I was a teenager a friend invited me to spend the night at his house. I accidentally walked into the wrong bedroom one day and found that my friend's mother and father slept in separate beds. After a year or so he ended up moving out of the bedroom, and into another room altogether. They obviously started out together in one bed, moved out of one bed into separate beds in the same room, to out of that room altogether. A process. Although I can't tell you the exact details or the why's of how it all happened, I will tell you the result was separation and divorce. When I got older, the father told me that his wife refused to have sex with him after birthing their children. Was a lack of intimacy and sex the problem? Maybe so. But one thing I know is that a healthy, regular, mutual intimacy in a marriage is very important.

I periodically wondered how the process of not sleeping together started. I mean how can you be with the one you love and not want to be intimate with them. Was it neglect, discouragement, or perhaps resentment on the part of the wife? We all desire physical connection, so how does cutting that off lead you to believe your marriage will be successful? It's like telling someone you'll take them out to a restaurant, but they can't order food. Instead, we have sex once every couple of weeks, or when it's time to get pregnant. It becomes this chore. You no longer look at your partner wanting to rip their clothes off, but rather instead, dread the thought. That's not crazy to you? It's not just boredom that stops sex from happening. Everywhere you look, there are pictures of men and women half naked, and some look better than your husband or wife. So that becomes desirable. It's in your face every single day and if you do not have integrity, honor, and strength, you too, can fall into this false sense of missing out because your spouse doesn't look like that model you saw on the billboard, or that actor you saw on the screen, or even that neighbor who moved in next-door. It's no wonder insecurities loom so largely these days. You literally have to be *perfect* to keep someone attracted to you. Meanwhile, what your lover should really be attracted to is your heart. Maybe if you felt that connection beyond a physical level, you would realize a renewed sexual attraction. I will cover the subject of intimacy in the following chapter.

4. Financial Pressure

Years ago, it didn't cost more than $200,000 for an education. It also didn't cost $500,000-plus for a home. The cost of living was very different from what it is now. You'd be naive to believe this fact doesn't cause strain on marriages today. There is no doubt that in the last 30-40 years, dynamics have changed. The economy and "keeping up with the Jones's" are driving both husband and wife to work full time jobs. You need to find a job to pay for student loans, a mortgage, utilities, living expenses, a baby, not to mention all the in-betweens. Problem is, it's extremely difficult for a single provider to find a job that can offer an income that will help you live comfortably while paying all of these bills, especially if you're in your mid 20's to 30's.

If we are not very careful, this strain causes separation between us. It halts us from being able to live life in peace. We're too busy paying bills to enjoy our youth. Forget going to dinner, you have to pay the rent or mortgage. You'll have to skip out on an anniversary gift this year because those student loans are due at the end of the month. Vacations? Not happening. We're trying to live the way our grandparents and parents did in a world that has put more debt on our plate than ever before. It's possible, but it puts us in an awful position. Part of life is being able to live. Not having the finances to do so takes away yet another important aspect of our relationships. It keeps us inside, forced to see the life everyone else is living. A solid budgeting plan and good stewardship has become a must in order to navigate through our present economy. Another added pressure is that many today have not been taught how to steward/manage their money properly. Priorities seem to be out of whack. Through many years of pastoring my church, I have noticed that people would choose a trip to an amusement park, or purchase new designer shoes, or frequent expensive restaurants rather than pay their bills or tithe to the church. Then at the end of the day, when there's not enough to pay bills, they feel that God has abandoned them. There must be Biblical principles at work in the life of a believer wanting to live a financially stress-free life. Financial pressure places stress on marriages.

Emotional Affairs and Their Warning Signs

One of the best definitions on emotional adultery that I have heard is: "Friendship with the opposite sex that has gone too far is unfaithfulness of the heart..., sharing things with the opposite sex that should only be reserved for your spouse." Emotional adultery is the reaction of two hearts, the chemistry of two souls. It is an unlawful connection with someone other than your spouse.

Here is a list of indications of Emotional Affairs:

1) You greatly anticipate being with this person.
2) You pay special attention to grooming and hygiene when you know you will be around this person.
3) Your eye contact is deep and prolonged; your eyes lock in an unusual way.

4) Your relationship with this person is secretive without your mate's full knowledge.

5) You discuss your marital problems with this person or vice versa.

6) You find yourself being alone with this person on a frequent basis.

7) This person listens to you better than your spouse.

8) This person seems to know, understand, respect, or appreciate you more than your spouse.

9) You cannot imagine what life would be like without this friend.

10) Casual touching or affection is a normal part of this relationship.

I agree to become totally accountable to my spouse in the area of emotional affairs by allowing and taking heed of my spouse's observations and warnings. I agree to completely extinguish chemical reactions that have begun or may begin in the future.I agree to disclose to my spouse any future struggles at their first appearance.

King Solomon, the wisest man who ever lived said,

"Can a man take fire in his bosom, And his clothes not be burned? Or can a man walk on hot coals, And his feet not be scorched? So is the one who goes in to his neighbor's wife; Whoever touches her will not go unpunished.

- Proverbs 6:27-29

Reminds me of a moth fatally attracted to the light. It burns the wings off the moth while still in flight. Are your wings on fire? Marriage falling apart, losing the respect of your kids and family, and you seem to be able to pull away from the scorching light still walking on hot coals? Recognize that an intimate relationship with someone outside of your marriage is a fatal attraction, and will result in your getting burned. So, how can we avoid the "D" word? Answer: Guard the garden that God has placed you in. Place a *high value* on your marriage.

Be courageous and strong concerning your marital commitment. Develop a strong relationship with the Lord and learn to apply His principles and guidelines. Read books dealing with marriage and highlight points that speak into your life and need attention. Develop and maintain a regular prayer life. Attend a church that challenges your thinking and causes decisions to be made on your part. Work hard to shore up your weaknesses through an honest self-evaluation along with open, honest, reliable communication with your spouse. Remove the escape hatch called divorce and remove the "D" word from your vocabulary.

Please take time to pray this prayer:

Lord Jesus, I close the escape hatch called divorce and look to you as the answer to any and all problems that I encounter in my marriage. Give me discernment, common sense, and strength whenever tempted to be unfaithful to my spouse. Help me to identify and appreciate the inner beauty of my spouse and not get caught up in overemphasizing the outward. I come against selfish desires within me and will not be caught up in social media to a point where it undermines the sanctity of my marriage and private life. Bless my finances and help me to put you first with my tithe and offerings. I pray all of this in the name of my Lord and Savior Jesus Christ. Amen.

Chapter 8
An Affair-Proof Marriage: A How-To Guide

ONE OF THE key ways to affairproof your marriage is to set up boundaries that will help safeguard against potentially dangerous situations. In the Bible, Job cautioned men not to lurk at your neighbor's door *(Job 31:9)*. Twice in Proverbs a clear warning is sounded about keeping far away from a seductive person.

> Keep to a path far from her, do not go near the door of her house.
>
> - Proverbs 5:8

> Do not let your heart turn to her ways or stray into her paths.
>
> - Proverbs 7:25

Remember, Potiphar's wife made a sexual advance towards Joseph when no one was around *(Genesis 39:11)*. Here are some suggested boundaries you and your spouse could agree upon to protect your relationship from harm:

1) Never get involved in one-on-one counseling with members of the opposite sex.
2) Never discuss sexual issues with members of the opposite sex, even on the phone.
3) Never enter a home of a member of the opposite sex alone.
4) Never get into a vehicle with a member of the opposite sex (unless your spouse or sibling is present). This would include errands, favors, babysitters etc.

5) Never have a member of the opposite sex in your office/room unless the door is open or if there is a window view.

6) Never have lunches or coffee breaks alone with a member of the opposite sex.

7) Never work after hours with just you and a member of the opposite sex.

8) Never discuss personal marriage problems with members of the opposite sex.

9) Never travel on business alone with a member of the opposite sex.

10) Never flirt or make sexually suggestive comments.

11) Be careful about touching members of the opposite sex. Tight extended hugs, hand squeezing, hair stroking can all send the wrong message.

12) Use great discretion in answering cards and letters from members of the opposite sex. Allow your spouse to review the correspondence. Try to include your spouse's name and positive words about your spouse in return correspondence.

13) Here it is - always make your cell phone available to your spouse. Surrender passwords etc. to your spouse when asked. Never text anything that you wouldn't show your spouse.

Most today would consider these boundaries archaic or ridiculous even. But they are healthy safeguards that, if applied, will drastically reduce the chances of extramarital affairs. When asked for help, I have referred to some of these principles only to have the person/couple look at me in shock. One actually responded with, "We are adults and don't need to police one another." Yet the reason they were in my office in the first place was to get help, and try to salvage a damaged relationship. Many of the boundaries had been crossed and eventually led to adultery. Which of these boundaries are already in place in your marriage? Which ones need to be put into place now? Without good boundaries, true intimacy between you and your soulmate is impossible. If I had a dollar for every wife who shared with me in counseling that they had difficulty having sex with their husband because there has been a breach in trust due to their experiencing intimacy with another woman, I would be rich. The result of one or the other sharing themselves emotionally with another outside the marriage has taken intimacy and turned it into resentment. It is very difficult for a woman to share themselves with their husbands after he has crossed the line with another person. Resentment is an automatic turn-off sexually and emotionally.

The enemy of true intimacy is a man with little or no boundaries. You must join in agreement to have all of these boundaries present in your marriage that you might be above reproach. Safeguard your marriage. Having an affair doesn't usually start with sex. Typically, there are mental steps that take place, followed by physical steps which eventually lead to an affair. You may hear people say, 'It just happened...one minute we were friends then the next thing I know, we are having an affair." These people didn't pay attention to the warning signs. They didn't actively take steps to avoid the inevitable affair, and they are now emotionally and physically invested in another person outside the marriage. Make your marriage adultery-proof by determining boundaries that you have with the opposite sex. Boundaries are in place to protect you from going too far. They are important to establish to ensure your marriage is safe and protected. If you already have relationships that sound similar to the above situations then you need to cut it off *now*.

If you find this to be a struggle, then you need to ask yourself why. If he/she is just a friend, then why can't you give up on that relationship to save your most important relationship, your marriage? Remember, most people who have affairs never thought that they would be the one to have an affair. If you truly value your marriage, then you will protect it. Love isn't just about feelings, it is intentional and it takes effort. Remember that all relationships have problems, and while an affair may start off feeling great, the newness will fade and the baggage will collect, leaving you feeling unsatisfied once more. If you were to see an off-ramp sign on the freeway that says "do not enter," would you resent it or would you appreciate it? God says if you play by His rules, you'll come out a winner and enjoy longevity in your marriage.

"You shall not commit adultery"
- Exodus 20:14 (The 7th of The 10 Commandments)

What is adultery? Sexual intercourse between a married person and a partner other than husband/wife. Then Jesus steps in with the New Testament and elaborates on the meaning of adultery by saying that we can commit adultery simply by having another in our imaginations (heart). Why? Because He created us, and what He knows about sin is that it starts from the heart. We see it, desire it, then we act it out. God wants us to use sex as a tool for *building* a marriage not destroying it.

> "Husbands and wives must be faithful to each other. God will judge those who are immoral and commit adultery."
>
> - Hebrews 13:4

Steps to Avoid the "D" Word

1. Address problems with your spouse.

When we don't talk about what's bothering us, we tend to want to find someone's shoulder to cry on. *Be careful* about discussing your marital problems over and over again with someone who *isn't* your partner.

2. Be involved in your partner's life.

Learn all you can about what makes each other tick. Make sure to create fun and meaningful times with your spouse. If there is little or no involvement with your spouse, it makes it that much easier to look elsewhere for fulfillment.

3. Keep the home fires burning.

Feeling desired may increase a woman's libido. Engage with your partner to make sure she feels wanted and knows that you're still attracted to her. Since the brain loves novelty, it's easy to get sidetracked by the new guy or girl, especially if she (or he) is not getting attention at home. Keep love alive through frequent compliments and good ol' fashioned romance.

4. Don't air the dirty laundry.

Whether you're sharing marital complaints with your coworker at the office or with an online friend of the opposite sex, you may be setting the stage for an emotional affair.

When you're sharing more with a friend of the opposite sex than you do with your mate, you've crossed that line. Add in some physical attraction and you may even be heading towards a physical affair.

5. Keep work relationships nine-to-five.

If you're meeting after work or grabbing dinner, perhaps you should invite your husband or wife along. Transparency is everything and may keep the relationship in the friend zone.

6. Beware of crossing the line.

Catch yourself if you're treading into dangerous flirting territory. Consider if you'd be okay with your spouse sharing a slightly NSFW (not safe for work) email or joke. There may be no sure way to affair-proof a marriage like you would child-proof the cabinets, but you can lessen the chances with regular communication and trying to meet each other's needs, both emotionally and sexually. It's easy to fall into the pattern of being too exhausted or distracted after work or a day spent chasing after the kids. But, staying attentive to each other is essential to maintaining intimacy.

More Tips on How to Protect Your Marriage

1. Make your marriage commitment known.

Affirm it to your friends and the people you work with so there's no doubt about where you stand on this issue). How? For starters—wearing your wedding ring. Make sure that your conversation reflects the fact that you are happily committed to your marriage. Another way you can make your commitment known is to show photos of your spouse, family, special occasions etc. By doing these things you are communicating:

1) I'm not available.
2) I'm off the market.
3) I am a non-negotiable item.
4) Don't even think about it.

If someone gives you their phone number, don't stick it in your pocket! I know it feeds your ego: "Wow, after all these years, I've still got what it takes." Throw it away, or better yet, don't accept it—publicly affirm your commitment.

2. Magnify the consequences.

Here is my favorite approach developed by Pastor Rick Warren. I have applied this step to countless people in counseling: Think of what it might cost you once you are caught in an adulterous affair. Remind yourself of the devastation and destruction that is caused by it.

> "The one who commits adultery is an utter fool, for he destroys his own soul."
>
> > - Proverbs 6:32

Many years ago, Pastor Jack Hayford preached a sermon I will never forget titled: "Why sexual sins are more devastating than others." In this sermon, he basically answered the question of why the consequences of sexual sins are more devastating than other sins with the fact that it often involves other people. In other words, there is collateral damage. On a personal level, nothing damages emotions like sexual sin. Sexual sin leaves permanent scars. The shame just doesn't seem to go away. We try to cover the shame, but it haunts us even years later. The sense of loss to everyone involved is enormous. As a pastor and family counselor, I can't tell you how many people I've talked to that have said, "I wish I could just turn the clock back. I wish I could just erase it and start over."

> "A man can hire a prostitute for the price of a loaf of bread, (cheap trick) but adultery will cost a man all he has"
>
> > - Proverbs 6:26, GNT

We're not talking about losing money, but the loss of what the Jews called *hispa* – life, dignity, honor, respect. Ask anyone who has been caught in adultery how it was. They never say "Oh it was fantastic." Instead, "It wasn't worth it, it cost too much." The cost of repairing your marriage and making it work is always lower than the cost you'll pay for adultery. This is why I highly suggest that a good attempt of reconciliation takes place before deciding to pull the plug. Having an affair just doesn't pay in the long run. Everybody loses (spouse, kids, friends, etc.). Remember: God put this commandment in here for our benefit. I've been married to my wife for over 40 years and in those years, she has been the only woman I have known sexually. By God's grace I intend to be faithful to her for as long as I live. Why?

Four huge reasons:

1) I love Jesus Christ.

Jesus said, "If you love *Me*, keep *My* commandments."
God says '*No*' to sex outside of marriage.

2) I love my wife and kids.

I have carried the pain of a broken home; I didn't want to risk that for my kids.

3) I fear the judgment of God.

I think it is a healthy fear that one ought to have.
Spiritual death = separation from God Sin separates you from God!

4) I value the ministry and all of the people God has placed in my sphere of influence.
I don't live just for myself. Good people depend on my character, integrity, etc.

Due to the culture that we live in, there must be a concerted effort by all who value the marriage covenant to maintain a pure relationship with our spouse. Never before in my lifetime have I seen so many opportunities to sin. I mean really, only a few years ago you would have to hunt down a place that offered pornography, vile movies and sexually implicit entertainment. Now, it's right there at the tip of your fingers. Yes, the keyboard provides a much too easy access to things that will tear down and potentially destroy everything God wants to establish in your life and marriage. The attack is fierce and I find myself counseling couple after couple who have fallen due to this type of exposure and involvement. Without a deep sense of commitment, moral values and a strong discipline, almost anyone can fall prey to the onslaught of this present world. What must one do to affair-proof a marriage? There is not just one answer to that question, but I remember back to 1974 when I gave my life to Jesus Christ. One of the first verses I learned and memorized was,

"Walk in the spirit and you will not fulfill the lust of your flesh."

- Galatians 5:17

One of the main reasons I place so much emphasis on Biblical references throughout this book is because without morals or absolutes, people will inevitably draw their own lines. People who do not hold to godly principles will find themselves attempting to recreate God's order of things (which is impossible) on their own terms and will always result in confusion and frustration. God has blessed the institution of traditional marriage which is designed to be one of the greatest joys in the world. Marriage, when lived out with dignity, is fun, rewarding, deep and among the most fulfilling relationships known. Take every step possible to affair-proof your marriage.

Please take time to pray this prayer:

Heavenly Father, I confess and repent of the sin of adultery (because the Bible tells us that even lusting after someone in our minds is a form of adultery), and I ask that you forgive me of this sin. In the name of Jesus, and by the power of His blood, I now renounce, break and sever all unholy soul ties formed. I now command any evil spirits which have taken advantage of this unholy soul tie, to leave me now in the name of Jesus! Lord God, help me to maintain solid boundaries that will protect the integrity of my relationship with my spouse. Give me discernment when it comes to seductive spirits and help me to run from sin. I pray that the spirit of this present world will have no power over me or my spouse. I am determined to maintain healthy relationships, never crossing the line or exposing myself to enticement. Lord, help me to magnify the consequences of sin in my mind and heart. I pray all of this in the name of my Lord and Savior Jesus Christ. Amen.

Chapter 9
How to Build and Maintain Intimacy

WHAT IS INTIMACY? Well, that depends on whether you ask the question to the husband or the wife. I know I have said this before, but most men do not know what intimacy really is until they are about forty years old. Prior to that, it only means one thing and one thing only: sex. But as men mature and grow in relationship with their wives, they should come to realize that intimacy is really "Into Me You See." The ability to see into the heart and emotions of their life partner. It is pillow talk, reading between the lines, knowing that there is something special about spending time together and the ability to embrace without it always leading to sex. Most women live through marriage with an intimacy deficit. Husbands would be wise to learn their wives' love language and speak it fluently. What is the key to intimacy? Well, one is good communication. Jesus Christ is the master of communication. On many occasions, our Lord used self-disclosure in conversing with His disciples. Jesus thought it was important to become transparent and talk about what He was feeling, good or bad.

Note the following examples:

1) I sensed that power went out from me (Luke 8:46).

2) You unbelieving and perverse generation, how long shall I be with you, and put up with you? (Luke 9:41a).

3) I have earnestly desired to eat this Passover with you before I suffer… (Luke 22:15)

4) You are those who have stood by me in my trials (Luke 22:28).

121

5) But I have a baptism to undergo, and how distressed I am until it is accomplished... (Luke 12:50),
6) My soul is deeply grieved to the point of death. Remain here and keep watch with me... (Matt. 26:36)
7) Now my soul has become troubled, and what shall I say? "Father, keep me from this hour?" (John 12:27).

The Apostle Paul was also a gifted communicator who was very transparent about his innermost thoughts and emotions. All of these expressions of self-disclosure come solely from one book of the Bible: 2 Corinthians. These "snapshots of the soul" are provided below in summary form:

1:6 - If we are *distressed*.
1:8 - Hardship 'we *suffered*.
1:8 - Under *great pressure*.
1:8 - We *despaired* even of life,
1:9 - In, our *hearts we felt* the sentence of death.
2:1 - I made up my mind 1 would not make another painful visit to you
2:2 - If I *grieve* you ...
2:4 - I wrote to you out of *great distress* and *anguish of heart*.
2:13 - I still had *no peace of mind*.
4:1 - We do not *lose heart*,
4:8 - We are *perplexed* but not in despair.
5:2 - We *groan*
6:10 - Regarded ... as *sorrowful*, yet always *rejoicing*
6:11 - We have *spoken freely* and *opened wide our hearts* to you. We are *not withholding affection* from you.
7:4 - I am *greatly encouraged*
7:8 - *My joy* was greater than ever.
7:9 - Yet now I *am happy*.
7:13 - We were *especially delighted*.
10:9 - I do not want to seem to be trying to *frighten* you with my letters,
11:1 - I hope you will put up with a *little of my foolishness*.
11:11 - Why? Because I do not <u>love You</u>? God knows *I do*.
11:28 - I face daily the *pressure of my concern* for all the churches.
12:11 - I have made a fool, of myself.
12:20 - I am afraid that...
12:21 - I am afraid that...

If Jesus and Paul felt it was important to communicate their thoughts and feelings, why shouldn't we? A key for great marital communication is to honestly relate to one another on an emotional level. These expressions need to be from the heart without blame or producing guilt. Husband and wife need to grant permission for self-disclosure and encourage it. *This* is intimacy.

Sexual Relationship

In *Song of Solomon 5:16,* the woman says, *"His* words are kisses, his kisses words. Everything about him delights me, thrills me through and through! That's my lover, that's my man…"

In the next chapter, this is what the man says in response:

"Dear, dear friend and lover, you're as beautiful as Tirzah, city of delights, Lovely as Jerusalem, city of dreams, the ravishing visions of my ecstasy. Your beauty is too much for me—I'm in over my head. I'm not used to this! I can't take it in. Your hair flows and shimmers like a flock of goats in the distance streaming down a hillside in the sunshine. Your smile is generous and full— expressive and strong and clean. Your veiled cheeks are soft and radiant. There's no one like heron earth, never has been, never will be. She's a woman beyond compare. My dove is perfection"
                                              - Song of Solomon 6:4-9

This is describing the kind of marital relationship that is possible to those who come together and share true intimacy. I want to talk to wives for just a moment, but husbands, don't tune out. Wives, I want to challenge your thinking. What would you think if I told you that God gives you permission (encourages you) to daydream about your husband's body? That's right, if you read the eight chapters of Songs of Solomon, you'll find a complete and thorough description of a man and a woman romancing each other, daydreaming, fantasizing about each other, sexually, physically. Does the very thought cause you to blush or roll your eyes and think, 'No way! I could never do that!'? Maybe there is little or no desire for such a thing. Why not?

Ladies, where do you get the idea that fantasizing about your husband is wrong? Maybe because we feel that these actions constitute lust. You know God's Word's and you know lust is wrong. Yet, the Song records Torah's sexual fantasies about her husband, and we're telling you it's alright. Why would God say it's okay for a wife to have sexual daydreams about her husband? Isn't that lust? The distinction happens with two words 1) husband and 2) wife. God gives permission for a wife to sexually daydream about her husband, and for a husband to daydream sexually about his wife. You may say: "I'm still not too sure about that!" Then why on earth would God Himself give us as part of the Bible the Song of Solomon?

I mean, as important as the Bible is, along with subjects like faith, prayer, redemption, history, spiritual warfare, doctrine, etc. Placed right here among all these critical subjects is the sexuality and romance of a husband and wife. Why? Because it is very much a part of God's order of things! A healthy, exciting sexual relationship is not only a concern to God but necessary for the health and well-being of any married couple. God urges us to ponder, dwell, delight in the gift of your spouse's body for you.

Allow yourself to become sexually aroused so you can enjoy ecstasy with your spouse. For you to fantasize sexually about anyone else, the neighbor down the street, the ex-boyfriend, the secretary at work with the low-cut blouse, sister in church, etc. *is* a sin. But your husband is part of you; God sees the two of you as one. In this oneness is freedom. God does not want us to abandon sexuality. He wants us to indulge in unrestrained joy and passion, and to intoxicate one another with delight. How's that for a description. His one boundary is this: *One* husband and *one* wife, in private for life. Within the context of this marriage relationship, God gives you permission to:

1) Be free with your words
2) Be free with your body
3) Be free in your mind.

Exclusively, with your mate.

Most couples I know want to experience sexual freedom with each other, but many are unable to because their minds are filled with junk. Listen to what couples had to say about it in a book *Intimacy Ignited*. In the book, a husband writes:

"I'm to the point where I feel convicted every time I make love to my wife. Because every time I do, a videotape of a women I was with before I got married parades across my mind. I feel like I'm committing adultery while I'm making love with my wife, Help!"

Has this every happened to you? Does this have to happen for you to be aroused with your wife? If so you must understand that according to Jesus Christ you are living in adultery! Adultery is a sin that erodes the fabric of the marriage covenant. Contrary to the world mindset this is not sexual freedom, it is bondage! Like the alcoholic – they're not sucking out of a bottle, it's sucking out of them! So, what can I do to change that?

This time, a couple named Beth and Max share their frustrations in the same book:

Beth
I can't even imagine what being free in my mind looks like. I had several sexual partners before I married Max. If I tried to do what Tirzah did, I'm afraid images of other men would flood my mind. That, combined with the guilt I feel over having had two abortions, keeps me from really enjoying sex. To me, sex equals pain. So I just don't think about it.

Max
Beth's not the only one who shuts down her mind. It's the only way I can function. When I was ten years old, a friend showed me some porn magazine. I came into marriage with a mind stuffed full of images if naked women. Although porn is not a part of my life now, every time Beth and I make love, I see page 63 or the centerfold from June. We became Christians after we married, and the more I see God's holiness the more disgusted I am with what floods my mind. I just don't know how to get rid of the junk. Like Beth, I shut down. I could never let my mind go and be free, because I don't trust where my mind would go.

Is not Beth and Max shutting down their minds to sex and joining a commune somewhere? God has a better way. He says Be transformed by the renewing of your mind (Romans 12:2). The Greek word for "transformed" in this passage is where we get our English word "metamorphosis." It's not turning over a new leaf, it involves total change, from the inside out. So, we are talking about a mind that is brand spanking new, like nothing you've seen before, a mind that has been so completely changed, it is barely recognizable. Beth and Max, actually ended up having a complete transformation of minds. What about you? Do you believe God can renew your mind? Maybe you were sexually abused and you believe the images from the past will always hunt you and hinder your sexual expression. Perhaps you did something, saw something, heard something, and it imbedded itself so deeply in your mind that you're convinced your thoughts on sex will always be tainted. Or you were possibly raised in a strict environment where you were constantly told, restrain yourself, deny sexual passion. You feel these years of conditioning make it impossible for you to ever be wild and expressive sexually. Wrong. Christ came to set us free.

John 8:32 says, *"You will know the truth and the truth will set you free."* The truth itself won't set you free, knowing the truth will set you free. The "truth" is personified in Jesus Christ. Your mind is like a computer. When you were born, God installed a directory called "sex" early on, and the directory was empty. Over time, however, files were added to the directory. Certain files were corrupted immoral messages or images, perverted acts contrary to God's word. Good files produced right thinking, and corrupted files produced wrong thinking. Over the years, the accumulation of these files developed attitudes that form your current views about sex. Everything you have been told about sex, everything you've seen, heard, done or that has been done to you have all been stored in your mind. If sex is tainted in your mind, if freedom seems impossible, it is because the corrupted files keep your mind from functioning as God intended. The way to get your mind working properly is similar to the steps involved in fixing a sluggish computer: Inventory the system, identify and remove corrupted files, and install new programs that will protect the system and increase performance.

Please take time to pray this prayer:

Holy Spirit, I ask You to bring to mind the action and images You want me to review for this period of my life. I give You permission to reveal anything I've suppressed or previously been unwilling to acknowledge. Search my heart. Expose what is hidden. I trust You to do this so I may be set free.

I'm going to shift gears now.

Get Rid of Porn

Pornography is dangerous, and is (in my opinion) the greatest attack on marriages in the 21st century. It wasn't too long ago that you'd have to get out and look for porn, but now it's literally a click away (internet). It requires true character and godly conviction and power to stay clear of it. Researchers now link changes in sexual behavior to the startling discovery that when people indulge in pornography, they release powerful chemicals that actually change the structure of the brain and body, creating a physical addiction. This addiction is so powerful it is being likened to cocaine, alcohol, and heroin. In a special report on love in marriage, *Time* magazine calls the internet "The crack cocaine of sexual addiction." According to psychologists and sociologists, pornography is transforming sexuality and relationships for the worse. Even secular psychologists are agreeing that pornography is destroying relationships. Pornography is a growing problem. Porn revenue is larger than all combined revenues of professional football, baseball, and basketball franchises.

In United States, revenue generated by the pornography industry exceeds the combined revenues of major television networks such as ABC, CBS, and NBC by $6.2 billion. Pornography generates $57 billion worldwide and $12 billion in the United States alone. Forty million adults regularly visit pornographic internet websites. Oh, and by the way, divorce in our country is at an all-time high. Coincidence? I think not. Richard Barry, president of the American Academy of Matrimonial lawyers, said pornography had an almost nonexistent role in divorce just fifteen or twenty years ago. Now, according to two thirds of the 350 divorce lawyers at a meeting of the American Academy of Matrimonial Lawyers, internet pornography played a significant role in divorces in the past year, with excessive interest in online porn contributing to *more than half* of such cases. Even secular people recognize the damage caused by pornography.

But the good news is that help for pornography addiction is available. Check out the following books: *Every Man's Battle: Winning the War on Sexual Temptation One Victory at a Time* by Stephen Arterburn, Fred Stoeker, and Mike Yorkey, and *An Affair of the Mind* by Laurie Hall.

When a man's eye wanders, you can't effectively legislate morality. The scripture says, *"verily, verily I say to you, you must be born-again."* It's not about turning over a new leaf, but being transformed by the renewing of your mind. How do you do that? The same way you break any addiction, compulsion, or obsession! Through the Word of God! That's right, by being brainwashed! Having your brain washed clean by the Holy Spirit. Every book I read that talks about transforming the mind says that I should memorize and meditate on God's words. Yes, you *know* it, but have you *done* it? This is what changes you! From personal experience, we know this to be true. Others also verify that their minds were renewed and healed when they *immersed* themselves in God's word and *committed* it to memory. Listen to Serena's story:

> "Six months ago, after my husband left for work, a man broke into my home and brutally raped me. I tried to make love with my husband, but the sights, the sounds, of the horror continued to run across my mind like a fast-forwarded videotape. I asked God to pull the violation from my mind. Then I began memorize one scripture verse each week for the next four weeks about the beauty of our sexual relationship with my husband. After asking God to transform my mind daily, last night we made love for the first time in eight months, and I didn't have any flashbacks."

The Word of God can reprogram our minds and make them new. The Holy Spirit is your virus protection program. He can alert you with a warning in your spirit when a virus is about to enter your mind. In that moment, you have a choice. You can quarantine files and later delete them so they do not affect your system, or you can ignore the warning and suffer the consequences.

How to Restore Romantic Love

James Dobson, a marriage expert, said: "Whenever something is presented repeatedly with a physically induced emotion, it tends to trigger that emotion all by itself." In other words, sometimes it's helpful (necessary) to act your way into a feeling. How many times have you started something and the "feelings" kicked in as you went along? A good example: "I didn't feel like going to church..." But you went anyway and ended up getting blessed out of your socks! Start "doing" before you "feel." Start asking your spouse what would make him/her happy again—with sincerity. Not with a "happy now?" "I can never please you," or "nothing makes you happy" kind of attitude. The scripture says,

"A man should fulfill his duty as a husband and a woman should fulfill her duty as a wife, and each should satisfy the other's needs"
- 1 Corinthians 7:3

You'll never experience fulfillment in marriage until you put others' needs before yours! Every so often I ask my wife, "How am I doing?" This is sometimes risky business because Liz will be very honest with me. It is at this vulnerable time that I feel as though my head is on the chopping block. Sometimes she tells me I'm doing great, and there are other times where she pulls out a chair. I know I'm in trouble when that happens, but it's all good because it ultimately leads to a healthy self-evaluation and good communication. You will never improve if you live in self-denial. Men, when do you feel most fulfilled as a husband? If you search deep inside your heart, you will probably discover that you feel most fulfilled as a man and husband when you take care of your wife and are a good covering for her!

Whenever Liz compliments my performance (in anything I do), I feel proud and have a deep sense of accomplishment and fulfillment. We men all want to believe we are that knight in shining armor. Ladies, how about you? When do you feel most accomplished as a woman and a wife? Isn't it when your husband's needs are being met by you and he compliments your endeavors? You would be surprised how far a good 'thank-you' or compliment takes you in your marriage. Intimacy is enhanced by doing the small things that mean so much to one another. So often our intimacy is interrupted by being rude, harsh, and abrasive to one another. When men's and women's needs continually go unmet, it becomes difficult not to "forsake all others." Although I stand by the truth that nothing justifies marital unfaithfulness, having a healthy intimate relationship dramatically reduces the chance of extramarital affairs. Here are a few scriptures on the matter.

"Give honor to marriage, and remain faithful to one another in marriage."

- Hebrews 13:4, NLT

"God will surely judge people who are immoral and those who commit adultery."

- 2 Timothy 2:22, NLT

"Run from anything that stimulates youthful lust. Follow anything that makes you want to do right. "God has called us to be holy, not to live impure lives. Anyone who refuses to live by these rules is not disobeying human rules but is rejecting God."

- 1 Thessalonians 4:7-8

And of course, there's always *our seventh commandment,*

"You shall not commit adultery"

- Exodus 20:14

Intimacy Tips

1. You need a healthy sex life, period.

"Let the husband render to his wife the affection due her, and likewise also the wife to her husband...The wife does not have authority over her own body, but the husband does... Stop depriving one another of sex."

- 1 Corinthians 7:3-5

Why does God say that? Because if done in love, there is no greater bond. Listen carefully wives: When a man agrees to an exclusive relationship with his wife, he depends on her to meet his sexual needs. If she fulfills this need, he finds in her a continuing source of intense pleasure, his love grows stronger. Don't misunderstand me however, love is a commitment and is not totally dependent upon the act of intercourse. When we age, things will change sexually, but the relationship should be deeper than ever before. However, as long as you are able to have sex and that need goes unmet, the opposite happens. He begins to associate her with frustration. If the frustration continues, he may decide she "just doesn't like sex" and just learn to live without it.

However, his strong need for sex remains unfulfilled. His commitment to an exclusive sexual relationship with his wife has now left him with the choice of sexual frustration or adultery. Unfortunately, some husbands resort to the latter. Still, some men never give in; they are able to make the best of it over the years. However, many do succumb to the temptation of an affair. Liz and I counseled a very young couple where the wife refused her husband regular sex. The very few times she would submit to it she would start crying during their time of intimacy. Although we tried on several occasions to get to the bottom of this abnormal response to her husband, we were unable to ascertain the reason. We had our suspicions, but the wife refused to allow us into the vault of her mind and history, so our hands were somewhat tied. One can only provide the right help if the full truth is communicated. Our warning: "If you continue to withhold sex from your husband without a good explanation, his frustration and the pressure will make things extremely difficult and add strain to the marriage. Having said that, I still want to go on record in saying that *nothing* justifies adultery. But again, the temptation to look elsewhere for sexual satisfaction is dramatically increased if a need as strong as this is constantly being denied. The sad reality of this story is that the husband fell in adultery, which led to divorce. Let's face it, part (and I emphasize the word "*part*") of the reason a man gets married is to fulfill a sexual need. If your husband wants sex, it should not be denied. I have never heard of one legitimate case of a forty-day headache.

Many a marriage can be saved by implementing this one rule alone. When you get married, you lose control of your body to your spouse. And it goes *both* ways.

Let the husband render to his wife the affection due her, and likewise also the wife to her husband. The

wife does not have authority over her own body, but the husband does. And likewise the husband does not have authority over his own body, but the wife does.
- 1 Corinthians 7:3-4

If your wife wants sex, it should not be refused either. If this need in either spouse is denied, it becomes unbalanced and resentment festers! *"Do not deprive one another except with consent for a time, that you may give yourselves to fasting and prayer; and come together again so that Satan does not tempt you because of your lack of self-control (v5).* Some of you ladies need to end your fast! Only Jesus fasted 40 days!

"Don't cheat each other of normal sexual intercourse...or you will expose yourselves to the obvious temptation of Satan"
- 1 Corinthians 7:5, GNT

There it is! You heard it from God! One of the reasons for adultery! Let me also add this very important point however. Part of your partnership of love should make way for understanding and empathy. If a wife refuses or has difficulty in the area of intercourse, many times, there is a valid reason for it. We have counseled some couples where the wife discloses the fact that she was molested or suffered other abuses that caused her to hold back sex with her husband. We have also had cases where the husband suffered sexual abuse and carried the scars and responses of that into their marriage. Love requires concern, empathy, patience, thoughtfulness, and understanding in these cases. It sometimes takes years of counseling, prayer, and sound communication to get the residual effects out of his/her system before experiencing the full freedom of intercourse.

2. In order to experience healthy marital intimacy, she needs conversation.

This need for good communication can be just as strong and important as a man's sexual need. Whenever you talk together in depth, honesty and openness (not found in conversation with others), she finds him to be the source of her greatest pleasure. When he refuses to give her the undivided attention she craves however, he becomes her frustration. In many cases, because of the husband's lack of interest in this area, she would rather have someone else take care of this important emotional need. I had no idea how big this need was until after my children got married and turned our home into an empty nest. Liz sat down on the couch with me and asked: "So, what do you want to do? Talk to me, what's on your mind, what did you do today, where should we go, let's talk…" I though in my mind, what do you usually do? I had no idea how much heat my daughter took off of me when they hung out at the house with their mother. I mean, they talked, shopped, laughed together, watched the same type of entertainment on the TV, etc. It had been a long time since it was just the two of us that I had forgotten how to fill all those gaps. I became aware that we need to adjust in every season of our lives. I have often wondered why so many seniors are getting divorced after so many years of marriage together. Could it be that their lives were built around school, sports, activities that they forgot to build a good, fulfilled relationship with each other? For some wives, they just live in frustration over it, and for others, this is a perfect recipe for an affair on her part. Seasons change and so must our approach to relationships.

"Reliable communication permits progress."
- Proverbs 13:17

Notice the scripture says "progress."

3. His needs are *not* her needs.

Let's continue answering the question I mentioned earlier: What could your spouse do for you that would make you the happiest or fulfilled?" There could be tons of answers to that question, but let me share with you what I feel are the most popular responses. They are classified in 10 Emotional Needs:

1) Admiration
2) Affection
3) Conversation
4) Domestic Support
5) Family Commitment
6) Financial Support
7) Honesty and Openness

8) Physical Attractiveness
9) Recreational Companionship
10) Sexual Fulfillment

Obviously, the way to keep a husband and wife happily married is for the husband and wife to meet the needs that are most important to the other. Except...those needs are very different. As a matter of fact, of the ten basic emotional needs listed, the five that are *most important* for the *wife* are usually *least important* for the *husband*. And the ones *most important* for the *husband* are *least important* for to the *wife*.

The reason marriages are in such trouble is that we have the tendency to think that meeting the needs of my partner is simply doing the things I like to do or what fulfills me. Clearly, that should not be the case.

"Show your love by being helpful to each other."
- Ephesians 4:2

When time and effort is spent meeting the needs of your spouse even before your own, that is what really demonstrates your love for one another. Experts discovered that if they flash the color red and gives you an electric shock, and then flashes the color green and gives you a soothing back rub, eventually the color red will upset you and green will relax you. We all could use less shock and more back rubs in our lives. That will restore romantic love! Become experts at meeting each other's needs. This is where your energy should be spent. This doesn't mean gritting your teeth and making the best of something you hate. One spouse should never suffer to meet the emotional needs of the other. Instead, it means learning how to enjoy meeting emotional needs that are low on your list of priorities. I love the quirks. There were certain things Liz would do in the early years of my marriage that used to make me impatient and edgy. I now love those things about her. Did she change? No, I did! Read and memorize scripture which is timeless and always relevant. Once you have installed the Word of God in your mind and given the Holy Spirit control over your thinking, you are ready for exciting possibilities. Freedom awaits you! In the joy of that freedom, you will learn a secret: You can use your mind to shift your body into a healthy sexual gear.

Shift into Sexual Gear

Gayle was diagnosed with advanced stage-three breast cancer at age forty. For the next ten months, she endured every kind of cancer treatment offered: five rounds of high dose chemo, stem cell replacement, radiation, and mastectomy even. As a result of all the treatment, she was menopausal and had one breast, no ovaries, and no uterus. Afterward, the cancer was gone, but so was her sex drive. "I couldn't believe that God would heal my body but then leave me in a condition in which I felt nothing sexually. But with God's help, I have learned how to shift my mind into sexual gear and now can ready my body for my husband. I have a deep passion for him that I never have had before. I find my desire is frequent if I am willing to shift my mind into gear. If this works for me, I know it can work for anyone," Gayle shared.

> "Let God transform you into a new person by changing the way you think"
>
> - Romans 12:2, NLT

Max, Beth, Serena, Gayle and other examples of deliverance are all stories of people made new after applying God's Word and power in their lives. You too, can act differently and feel differently. Truthfully, this process may take time. For some it has taken years. Even though we have outlined a few practical and helpful steps, setting your mind free is not about a program but about Jesus Christ. Trust Him. He wants your mind to be free even more than you do! Ask Him, trust Him, and don't be surprised if He accomplishes something far beyond your wildest dream. You may be asking: 'Why so much time spent on the subject of pornography in a chapter titled intimacy?' Well, nothing violates true, heartfelt intimacy more than adultery and pornography.

Allow me to introduce a term that I call *The Ephesians 5 Principle*:

Wives, submit to your own husbands, as to the Lord. For the husband is head of the wife, as also Christ is head of the church; and He is the Savior of the body. Therefore, just as the church is subject to Christ, so let the wives be to their own husbands in

everything. Husbands, love your wives, just as Christ also loved the church and gave Himself for her...
                                                                    - Ephesians 5:22-25

Almost every time I minister at a marriage retreat gathering, at least one or two wives anonymously submits a note with this question on it: "Am I bound by scripture to do whatever my husband wants me to do sexually?" My answer: If what he asks you 1) violates scripture, or 2) violates your conscience, you are not bound to submit to it. *The Ephesians 5 principle* is applied like this: If the husband loves his wife anything near the way Christ loves the church (*"Husbands, love your wives, just as Christ also loved the church and gave Himself for her" (v25).*), then he would never ask you to do anything that harms or hurts you emotionally, physically, or makes you feel dirty, sinful, shameful or guilty.

A husband must always consider the feelings of his wife, and not demand his way at the expense of her peace and security. If and when the husband honors the feelings of his wife by not demanding his own way sexually, the wife responds positively to the fact that he has placed her feelings above his own. The result—this husband then becomes a person where submission comes much easier, and in some cases a pleasure rather than an act of stringent obedience or submission. If you come to know the love that God has for you, and that His plans are not to harm you but to prosper and bless you, then submitting to such a God is never grievous but pleasurable. We serve and submit to a God who loves us and places our health and well-being above all else. Husbands, find the fulfillment in loving your wife like Christ loved the church. Likewise, wives, find the satisfaction in submitting to such a man. Have you ever sensed the affection of the Lord upon you in a time of prayer, worship or meditation on Him? A similar result is experienced by the wife when the husband is affectionate toward his wife.

Having said that, there is also instruction to the wife concerning her sexual response to her husband:

A man should fulfill his duty as a husband, and a woman should fulfill her duty as a wife, and each should satisfy the other's needs. A wife is not the master of her own body, but her husband is; in the same way a husband is not the master of his own body, but his wife is. Do not deny yourselves to each other, unless you first agree to do so for a while in order to spend your time in prayer; but then resume normal marital relations. In this way you will be kept from giving in to Satan's temptation because of your lack of self-control.

- 1 Corinthians 7:3-5 (GNT)

Again, when the Bible tells a woman to submit to and honor her husband, it should never be done at the high cost of feeling dirty or to demean you, but to give you the keys that open the door of your hearts toward each other. Scripture is also instructing the wife to yield and submit to her husband's physical needs and desires. It is very important that this exchange of love, honor and submission finds a healthy balance and fortifies the relationship. The reciprocity aspect of the *Ephesians 5 Principle* is there to establish trust and intimacy in your marriage.

"A man should fulfill his duty as a husband and a woman should fulfill her duty as a wife, and each should satisfy the *other's needs.*

- 1 Corinthians 7:3 (Italics Mine)

You will never experience fulfillment in marriage until you put the others' needs before yours! James Dobson's words are worth repeating: "Whenever something is presented repeatedly with a physically induced emotion, it tends to trigger that emotion all by itself." In other words, sometimes it's helpful (necessary) to act your way into a feeling. How many times have you started something and the "feelings" kicked in as you went along? An example I shared earlier was the thought, 'I don't feel like going to church...' entering your mind. But you went anyway, and ended up getting blessed out of your socks! Earlier, I also mentioned the importance of asking your spouse what would make him/her happy again—with sincerity. Not, "happy now?" "I can never please you." "Nothing makes you happy." We must learn to identify and respond to each other's needs.

Men, when do you feel most fulfilled as a husband? When you take care of our wife! You come into God's order of things when you rise to be her "covering, priest, protector." Ladies, when do you feel most fulfilled as a wife? When you live in security, love, and sound communication. Another important aspect of a healthy marriage is your willingness and ability to build one another. David Zinczenko shares a few examples on how you can do so on a day to day basis:

10 Compliments That Wow a Man

1. "Your arms are definitely looking bigger."

Men can be just as paranoid about the way their bodies look as women can be. In fact, nearly 90 percent of men in a national Men, Love & Sex survey say there's at least one body part they'd like to change (42 percent saying they want a new gut). While men don't necessarily want women to lie if they're out of shape, it never hurts to notice he's looking good...or at least trying to look better.

2. "Ha ha ha ha ha ha ha."

Guys spend all of high school, the better part of the work day, and at least 12 times a day via e-mail trying to make people laugh. Because men value their sense of humor as one of their most important qualities, a hearty, genuine laugh is as flattering as it gets.

3. "Wow."

Doesn't matter whether it comes as he's getting undressed or after you've finished having sex, this short, sweet word (best done in a whisper) may just be the ultimate ego-stroke. A picture may say a thousand words, but this three-letter word sums up roughly 10,000 of them.

4. "You the man."

Guys hear this all the time. From *other guys*. They hear it at work, on the golf course, and when one dude from the group buys drinks for everyone. But if it comes from a woman—no matter the context—the message is that, "Hey, you and I are buddies, too." Which is actually pretty darn sexy.

5. "The kids just adore you."

More than 50 percent of men say that their families—
more so than work and salary—are what defines them most as
men. So when a woman affirms that he's a family hero, it's a
compliment that stretches way beyond anything you could ever
say about his haircut.

6. "What do you think?"

We've all seen it a million times with long-married couples:
They engage in cerebral power struggles, where neither can
concede on anything. Whether it's the best way to move a piece
of furniture or the fastest way to reach the interstate, I'm not
saying that men should have the only say in decisions, but
some guys do feel like they actually have very little say.

7. "Meow."

The stats show that 61 percent of men think their partners
aren't sexually adventurous enough. While a feline one-liner
doesn't automatically qualify as adventurous, it does show a bit
of inhibition, and the message is one he likes to hear: That
perhaps he's brought a little bit of the animal out of you.

8. "Impressive."

Guys love feats. They love accomplishments. They love
being acknowledged for their strength, power, and, simply,
their masculinity. So a well-timed observation like this one,
whether it comes after he carries a TV to the family room, or
figures out a way to fix the pipes without having to call the
plumber, feeds into his need to feel like the family protector.

9. "I want you."

Women don't need to go on about a guy's eyes or hair or
clothes. What a guy really wants to hear is that he's the total
package, and this acknowledgement, whether it's referring to
bedroom behavior or relationship stability, is the ultimate
compliment of them all.

10. "I can't live without you."

Although co-dependence is not healthy, being reminded that you love, cherish and need him sure adds much to the relationship in the way of confidence and assurance.

10 Compliments That Wow a Woman

1. "You're the hottest girl in the room."

What women doesn't want to be viewed as that special beauty that stands out from the crowd? The fact that you believe that is a confidence booster and pays big after the time and preparation she invested.

2. "How to Lose a Guy in Ten Days is my favorite movie too!"

Men and women are definitely wired differently, and almost nothing drives this home more than movie selection. Sitting with her and enjoying what she enjoys will definitely provide her with a sense of assurance that *you care* about what she cares about.

3. "Wow, that looks good on you."

Noticing changes and add-ons will always bring a smile to her face and let her know that you appreciate her spending the time, effort and money to look her best.

4. "As long as you're there, I don't care where we go."

Corny? Never! Romance, romance, romance. What woman doesn't like to be the very center of a man's attention and love?

5. One wife asked her husband, "If you could change one thing about your life what would it be?" He responded, "I wish I would've met you sooner."

6. "Are you are losing weight?"

7. "You're my best friend."

8. "You have a lot of class."

9. "You make me a better person."

10. "You smell great."

Please take time to pray this prayer:

Lord, help me to experience true intimacy with my spouse. I renounce all manner of pornography and pledge my faithfulness to my spouse. Help me to find creative ways to show my love and admirations to my spouse and display appreciation each day. May my home be a place where compliments and affection flow freely. I pray that you will help me be patient. I pray all of this in the name of my Lord and Savior Jesus Christ. Amen.

Chapter 10
How to Build a Strong Team

IN ORDER FOR marriages to flourish, husband and wife must operate as a team. A team can be defined as "those who come together to achieve a common goal." When we think of a team, we usually refer to athletics. Teams that win must depend on everyone working together in harmony and fulfilling their particular responsibility. Words that come to mind when describing a good team are words like "unity, synergy, mutual commitment, strategy. When these terms are fully activated, they lead to a performance as one—a team—greater than the sum of the performance of its individual members. Marriage is a team! Henry Ford said, "Coming together is a beginning; keeping together is progress; but working together is success.". Our greatest achievements will be realized as we work together. Is your marriage team chaotic or fully functional? It is unrealistic to think that you can have a successful, fully functional, unified team when you have separate visions? This is called *division*. When you have division, the vision for your marriage will slowly fizz out. The only way our marriage will become all God designed for it to be is to work together in harmony with *His* principles. The Bible says:

> "Two are better than one, because they have a good reward for their labor. For if they fall, one will lift up his companion. But woe to him who is alone when he falls, for he has no one to help him up. The scripture tells us: "Two are better than one... because they have a good reward for their labor. And a threefold cord is not easily broken.
>
> - Ecclesiastes 4:9,10

If you don't get along, you can't go along.

"Can two people walk together without agreeing on the direction?

- Amos 3:3

Marriages are designed to function as a team.

Two Ingredients of Successful Teams

Most of you are familiar with the Biblical account of The Tower of Babel. What most people know is that God confused the language of those who were working on a huge construction project so they could not communicate what was necessary to complete the task. Let's first have a look at how they got God's attention.

"They said, 'Come, let us build for ourselves a city, and a tower whose top will reach into heaven, and let us make for ourselves a name, otherwise we will be scattered abroad over the face of the whole earth.' The LORD came down to see the city and the tower which the sons of men had built. The LORD said, 'Behold, they are one people, and they all have the same language. And this is what they began to do, and now nothing which they purpose to do will be impossible for them'"

- Genesis 11:4-6

How do we start a team? Here God saw the incredible power of people coming together working as a team. Notice that this construction team had a common goal and good communication. A successful marriage team is when you both have 1) a common goal; and 2) speak the same language. Throughout the chapter which records this effort, we find the words: "one people," "one mind," "one language," "one goal," "come," "let *us*." We read that God didn't like their purpose (evil), but He did acknowledge their ability to reach their goal. *The LORD said, "Behold, they are one people, and they all have the same language... and now nothing which they purpose to do will be impossible for them (v6).* Wow!

143

Basically, the scripture was saying that because they are united (one people), communicate well (speak the same language), nothing was impossible for them. How do you stop a team that is doing well?

"Come, let Us go down and there confuse their language, so that they will not understand one another's speech" (v7). So the LORD scattered them abroad from there over the face of the whole earth; and they stopped building the city (v8). Therefore its name was called Babel, because there the LORD confused the language of the whole earth; and from there the LORD scattered them abroad over the face of the whole earth (v9). How do you stop a team that is doing well? 1) Remove them from their goal (destroy their catalyst, the thing that causes them to work together); and 2) disrupt their communication (their ability to articulate the vision of that team). The result: "confusion"/eventual scattering! The moment your marriage loses a common goal and the ability to communicate with one another, the team is no longer effective. Being able to communicate with one another in just the right context is important too. Communication can differ even though we are working toward the same goal. "Secure the facility" means different things to different military agencies.

If you're in the Navy, it means to lock down the bulkheads. If you're in the Air Force, it means to lease the building with an option to buy. If you're in the Army, it means to make sure it is safe to enter. And if you're in the Marine Corp., it means to make a crater out of it. Again, be specific when articulating your concerns. A little while back I spoke to a former LAPD Division Chief about the Los Angeles civil unrest back in 1992. I found out that "cover me" meant different things to different agencies. To the LAPD, it means to watch with weapons drawn. To the National Guard, it means to just watch (because their weapons had ammunition). To the Marines, it means to spray bullets all around PD until they enter the building.

Remember that a healthy marriage team must have: 1) a common goal; and 2) good communication in order to be successful.

"Live together in harmony…"

- Philippians 2:2, Phillips

Harmony. Even Stevie Wonder and Paul McCartney sang about it in their song, 'Ebony & Ivory," where they sing, "…

ebony and ivory, live together in perfect harmony, side by side on my piano keyboard oh Lord why can't we…" Your marriage is the instrument that projects the chords produced by your relationship. It has been said that methods change but principles do not. When I look back at the great revival that Praise Chapel Christian Fellowship experienced back in the late 70's, there was a common thread to all other great moves of God. There was a common goal, clear communication, unity, and harmony. A team that works together, practices together, plays together, fights together, grieves together, rejoices together, partners together all share in the same prize together.

So, how can unity in marriages be enhanced? A good starting point is to cultivate an atmosphere of growth and maturity by finding common things you can agree upon. Make a list of priorities and review them regularly with one another. Ask yourself upon reviewing these priorities: are we making progress on those things that we agreed are important to both of us? Have your marriage shift towards more of a team approach. There Is No "I" In Team: This is an easy concept to lose if all we shoot for is what we want and don't place the right priority on our spouse's needs. Take a step back and ask yourselves: What are some changes you need to make to ensure that you and your partner operate as a team? On the next page is an exercise that should help point out strengths and weaknesses in your marriage. I use it often to help couples find where they are from their spouse's perspective.

Please be open and honest with your evaluation of your spouse. I made space for (10) likes and dislikes, so if you have more than (10), then go ahead and write it down on the back of your page or try to squeeze it in the best you can. The wife is to evaluate the husband and the husband will evaluate the wife. Do not allow your spouse to see what you are writing until both of you are finished.

Marriage Fire Code

Likes	Dislikes	
1.	1.	
2.	2.	
3.	3.	
4.	4.	
5.	5.	
6.	6.	
7.	7.	
8.	8.	
9.	9.	
10.	10.	

Likes	Dislikes
1.	1.
2.	2.
3.	3.
4.	4.
5.	5.
6.	6.
7.	7.
8.	8.
9.	9.
10.	10.

Marriage Fire Code

Evaluate Your Husband

Grade your husband on the following:

Affection (hugging, hand holding etc.)

A   B   C   D   F

Listening and responding to things you feel are important.

A   B   C   D   F

Accepting you for what and who you are.

A   B   C   D   F

Includes you in decisions that are made (consults you first).

A   B   C   D   F

Takes quality time with you regularly.

A   B   C   D   F

His/her ability to forgive and forget

A   B   C   D   F

Controls anger when things don't go his/her way.

A   B   C   D   F

OVERALL GRADE:

A   B   C   D   F

Evaluate Your Wife

Grade your wife on the following:

Affection (hugging, hand holding etc.)

A B C D F

Listening and responding to things you feel are important.

A B C D F

Accepting you for what and who you are.

A B C D F

Includes you in decisions that are made (consults you first).

A B C D F

Takes quality time with you regularly.

A B C D F

His/her ability to forgive and forget

A B C D F

Controls anger when things don't go his/her way.

A B C D F

OVERALL GRADE:

A B C D F

Please discuss your points (starting with the dislikes) and grades with each other, then exchange papers. Make the "dislikes" that were listed about you your prayer list for the week. Then pat yourself on the back for the "likes" that were written about you. Return after a few weeks and ask each other if they noticed an improvement on your part. Keep this evaluation and keep working on improving your grade.

Please take time to pray this prayer:

Lord, help me develop good communication and a clear vision for my marriage. I will view my marriage as a team, working together to build a life and marriage that will glorify God. I will be open to constructive criticism and tap into God's power to be the very best spouse I can. I will build a healthy prayer life and make decisions based on your Word and godly principles. I pray all of this in the name of my Lord and Savior Jesus Christ. Amen.